BAKHITA

BAKHITA

From Slave to Saint

By Roberto Italo Zanini

Translated by Andrew Matt

IGNATIUS PRESS   SAN FRANCISCO

Original Italian edition
Bakhita, Inchiesta su una santa per il 2000
© 2000 by Edizione San Paolo s.r.l.—Cinisello Balsamo, Milan, Italy

Cover photograph of Saint Bakhita

Cover design by Riz Boncan Marsella

There is but one sadness,
and that is for us not to be saints.

Léon Bloy

Only one who does not know the history of the Church
can feel ashamed of it,
because the history of the Church
is first and foremost
the history of the saints.

Alberto Zanini

CONTENTS

FOREWORD

I am very happy and honored to be able to offer to the Canossian family and to all their friends throughout the world the present volume on Josephine Bakhita, written on the occasion of her canonization.

I confess that I was deeply moved while reading these lively and stirring pages, which recount in a new way the story of a new saint. It is clear that the author was attracted by the mystery of her person—a mystery that comes alive in all those who have known her—even before meeting her, before admiring her extraordinary story, before understanding the message that her life always transmits, gently penetrating the soul of whoever listens with the "ear of the heart".

The attraction people feel for Mother Bakhita, "our universal sister", as Pope John Paul II called her, is truly exceptional. This attraction happened when she was alive, and it happens today, to people of the most diverse backgrounds. As the author makes very clear, Bakhita does not speak the language very well in which she communicates, she does not know many things, and she has done nothing extraordinary—but nevertheless many seek her out, many change their lives after coming to know her, many remember her with admiration and venerate her as the mediator of great favors from heaven. Why?

The secret springs from her profound relationship with the *Paròn*, the Lord—literally, "the Master". Bakhita is in constant dialogue with her Lord, entrusting herself to him with a childlike joy and intimacy at all times. Thanks to him, she becomes a master of humble and warm welcome to others, of joy, of goodness, of sincere forgiveness, of complete confidence in God, who has made her his daughter and thus free to welcome and give love, always and anywhere.

In our present age, in which efficiency occupies first place in the scale of values and mankind forces itself to suppress its yearning for authenticity and contact with the Eternal, Mother Bakhita demonstrates for us with authority that the greatest value is to become children of God and that only by "walking humbly with our God" (cf. Mic 6:8) do we fully discover our true and deepest selves.

May the memory of Mother Bakhita that is offered to us in these pages help us to grow in goodness and simplicity and in our capacity to read history, with its blessings and its burdens, in the light of Revelation. May we become ever-more-receptive sons and daughters in the hands of our Lord, who desires us to be signs of his love in the world—like Bakhita.

> Mother Ilva Fornaro
> Superior General
> Canossian Daughters of Charity

INTRODUCTION

I owe a debt to Bakhita. It is a little story, a personal story that led me to encounter this saint with the sweet smile and the deep, steady gaze. After learning about this woman, about her unique personality, which coincides with an equally unique charism of holiness, it becomes clear that her presence does not leave you. On the contrary, she accompanies you with a discrete persistence. Like an encouragement never to let the thread of providence slip from your fingers, a thread at times so tenuous and invisible, Bakhita helps us to make it through the labyrinth of our everyday struggles.

Bakhita is a friend, someone with whom you can share your disappointments and failures, someone you can ask for advice. Why? Because a woman who has survived the oppression of slavery does not set herself apart from anybody. Because listening to the whispers of suffering mankind continues to be the role most consonant with a woman who was the portress of the Canossian house in the town of Schio, Italy, who for years counseled and helped mothers worried about their children, who took countless little orphans by the hand, who aided fathers of families in finding work, who helped shelter soldiers in the convent, which was transformed into a hospital during the First World War. She, the "Little Brown Mother" who spoke the dialect of the people of the Veneto region in northern Italy, is ever close to those who might feel a little inadequate or tongue-tied speaking to the saints.

But let me return to my debt. I have to admit that what I, as a journalist, knew of Bakhita was linked to what unfolded before my eyes on the occasion of her beatification in 1992. At the time I knew nothing more than that the Sudanese slave who had become a Canossian nun had served as a cook, washed and folded the linens, and opened and closed the convent's front door for a little religious community in the province of Verezia. There was nothing extraordinary (like miracles, visions, or supernatural events), as might be expected for a blessed, I thought, without in any way judging the reasons that had brought her along the path toward canonization.

Then Bakhita came looking for me.

It happened after the death of Monsignor Claudio Sorgi, journalist, writer, TV personality, and above all a true priest, who died in November 1999 after a painful battle with a malignant form of lymphoma. Monsignor Claudio was the head of the missionary magazine for which I had worked over the course of many years. But he was also the author of several books, one of which was a biography of Josemaría Escrivá de Balaguer, *The Father*, written for the occasion of the beatification of the founder of Opus Dei, which took place on the same day as that of Bakhita.

At the beginning of his illness, Monsignor Claudio had accepted a commission from the Canossian Sisters to write Bakhita's life story. It was a commission he was unable to fulfill because of the relentless advance of his illness, which progressively deprived him of the use of his hands. Nevertheless, the book on Bakhita was his idée fixe. "You have to get better, Monsignor Claudio. You have to write the book. Bakhita is waiting", I would tell him when I visited him in the hospital.

One morning after his death, two Canossian sisters came to my office to ask whether he had left a completed manuscript or a draft of the book. Nothing; there was nothing.

But there I was. And the sisters proposed that I gather Monsignor Claudio's notes and pick up where he had left off. This was an inheritance, one that I could share only with the help of a friend, someone who was trained in the same school of journalism as I had been under Monsignor Claudio Sorgi. As a result, while strange circumstances gave us the impression that a plan was unfolding that was completely out of our hands, the baton of this task was passed on to Roberto Italo Zanini, one of the editors of the Catholic newspaper *Avvenire*. The time frame for completing the book was getting tight, and I, for family reasons, could no longer remain directly involved in the project. Yet, as I said before, I remained indebted to Bakhita.

The book, however, was written by Roberto. From the very start he set out with passion, beginning—as a good journalist should—even before he possessed all the facts about his subject. He soon did know his subject, of course, for he researched all the written records, traveled to the places where Bakhita lived, and visited and spoke with people who had known the saint in person. Among these living witnesses were women who, as young students at the Canossian-run school, strolled through the corridors and gardens in the company of the saint. Instead of recounting fairy tales, Sister Bakhita told them the adventures of her own life, with her voice that was a little hoarse. She walked with a particular gait that the girls of that time still remember.

The woman with chocolate-colored skin was affectionate, full of tenderness and kindness, which she concealed within the folds of a discretion that is pure humility. But Bakhita was also a strong woman, even stubborn, capable of responding with irony to laypeople and bishops alike. The only one who knew her through and through was the *Paròn*, her one and only true Master, with whom she was

13

in constant communication—whether in her mother tongue (possibly forgotten), in Arabic (taught to her by the slave traders), or in the dialect of the Veneto region, no one will ever know.

Indeed, this is of little importance because she is truly the "universal sister" whom Pope John Paul II raised to the altars and whose message knows no borders, received as it is by people of every race in countries all over the world.

Devotion to Bakhita has spread in an astonishing way in India, Brazil, and the United States (especially among African Americans), to name but a few places. Today Bakhita "sails" on the Internet, where many websites dedicated to her have sprung up. The black nun from the Italian province of Venezia hears prayers in many different languages, for people are not ashamed to open their hearts to someone who, as a slave, once stood on the lowest rung of the social ladder, beyond the pale of any caste system or hierarchy.

In her miracles, in her intercessions, Bakhita demonstrates daily that she is close to simple people, whose prayers come from the heart. In the prayers of those who suffer, sometimes hope gives way to bitterness, to resignation, to the dull turning in upon oneself. Bakhita knows how to receive even these splinters of suffering. She knows how to be a merciful sign of God's providence. And the affirmative power of her life has the effect of attracting even apparently indifferent persons to the faith, those who may be very far away yet who are receptive to the simplicity and humility of very small things that radiate truth.

As one who overcame great cultural, racial, and social distances in her life, Bakhita helps us in our own day to grasp the immense horizon of what it is that makes us truly free. Each one of us is a slave to something or to many things. We know it by the weight of the chains that still hold us in thrall, tethered to the earth, making us second-guess even those heavenly inspirations that stir our hearts most deeply. And Bakhita keeps repeating to each person she meets: Holiness is not an extraordinary event but rather a hope that belongs to everyone.

Miela Fagiolo D'Attilia

PROLOGUE

The room, white and unadorned, had a good, clean smell. The sheets on the remade bed were crumpled near the pillow, as if someone had just woken up. The bedspread shared the same undefined half-gray, half-blue color as hospital or hostel blankets. Everything was in its place, ready to come alive again in the hands of the one who had always used it.

A single ray of light entered diagonally through the window, cut across the room, and illumined a little tree made of metal wire and colored glass beads, resting upon the bedside table. The object was out of fashion, but "she made it", explained a young woman with pride, as she sat down beside the bed and seemed to pray. "She always liked to make things with beads, ever since she was in Venice", added the woman after a long pause, with a matter-of-fact air of familiarity, as if she were speaking about a friend or a relative.

That "she" obviously referred to the onetime owner of the room—the same person who must have occupied the wooden wheelchair tucked away in a corner. The wheelchair was a masterpiece of discomfort, the handiwork of a no-frills carpenter attentive to spending as little as possible on nothing more than the bare essentials. Even the tall and narrow bed left no room for any idea of comfort or beauty.

It was a small, uncomfortable room—uncomfortable like the little black wooden cross nailed to the wall above the pillow. Seated in a corner, the young woman rested her gaze upon it for a moment, after having carried on at length about the little tree and colored beads. Her lips, at first

17

motionless, now trembled slightly, revealing a muddle of thoughts interspersed with prayers.

The room was uncomfortable. And it was uncomfortable to remain standing there, but there were no other chairs. The impulse to leave had already come and been resisted: once, maybe twice.

The room lacked its owner, but the meager things that inhabited the room gave it a lived-in feeling. Standing there was physically uncomfortable, but comfortable in spirit.

This sounds like an empty catchphrase. But there was nothing there that one could even try to sell. Everything was bare and stripped clean, all except the improbable, multi-colored little tree. If there had been something to sell, it had been disposed of or given away, but it is unlikely that anything of the sort ever crossed the room's threshold.

People came and went. The flow of visitors was modest but constant—men, women, young families, the occasional nun or priest. All of them gave the impression of having come a long distance. People who were there for the first time and yet moved about as if they had always been there, as if they were at ease in the room that belonged to another.

A little Asian nun knelt at the bedside, remained there several moments, and then, furtively, without rising, slipped something under the pillow. When she stood up, she was smiling. She crossed herself and then left.

Grazed by the nun's black habit, the young woman seated by the bed was roused from her meditation. She bent down and with her hand searched in her purse next to her chair. After rummaging around a bit, she took out a card, an envelope, and a pen. The card looked like a greeting card. The young woman turned it over to the blank side and started writing. Her script was tiny—maybe so that she could fit in everything she needed to say.

Every so often the young woman stopped, remembered something, and began writing again. When there was no more room on the card, she turned it over and began filling up all the available space, even the little empty spaces around the printed letters of her name.

She paused again to recall one last thing. Then, with a slow-motion gesture completely alien to anyone used to fast-paced city life, the young woman placed her pen back in her purse. She took the envelope from her lap and inserted the card. Moistening her finger with saliva, she ran it across the adhesive flap and sealed it.

She was about to rise when, not yet satisfied, she turned to look for the pen in her purse again. Resting the envelope on her leg, on its cover she wrote no more than maybe two words.

Without even putting the pen back in her purse, the young woman got up from her chair. She came close to the bed. Raising the pillow slowly, as if trying not to disturb anything, she placed the card beneath it, then carefully tidied up everything. She paused again for a moment, standing, yet rocking gently to the rhythm of seemingly hidden music. Her knees touched and then drew back from the edge of the sheet that was turned over on the blanket.

Coming to herself again, the young woman moved away from the bed and turned to the chair. She picked up her purse, deposited the pen inside, straightened her clothes and her hair, crossed herself, and walked out the door.

The room remained empty, waiting for the owner who would certainly arrive—the little room that was both comfortable and uncomfortable, with its little tree of wire and beads and with its mystery under the pillow.

The chair was also empty. The angle of the sun had now shifted in the window. My legs hurt, but the desire to sit down had disappeared. Instead, my curiosity had grown.

Standing, the room, time. The time passed, and no one else came in. What was I doing during that time? Maybe I was praying. If reverent silence is prayer, then I was praying. I looked at the little tree. I looked at the pillow. I thought about the young woman's note, about all the time and the long, drawn-out gestures that went into writing it.

From down the corridor came the sound of distant voices. In the room that waited, nobody entered. I looked at the bed; I looked at the wheels under the worn-out wooden wheelchair. And then it hit me. I was the one for whom the room was waiting.

I waited for the courage to lift up the pillow. I waited for the courage because I thought I understood. I was the one for whom the room was waiting, not the owner. For the owner was the mystery under the pillow. The mystery was waiting for me. Just as it waited for the Asian nun and the young woman with the greeting card.

The writing was tiny and neat. Only two words: "For Bakhita". That is how it was written on the front of the small white envelope. And there were dozens more beneath it. More than a hundred, perhaps. Some notes had envelopes. Others were simply folded pieces of paper. There were a few postcards and many photos of families and babies. On some there was only her name. Others simply said, "Thank you". One was in Arabic, one in English, one in French. Two were in German. On one that was folded in quarters, a man asked for help about the lack of peace in his family. On a small sticky note, a woman expressed her gratitude: "Because since the last time I came to see you ..."

I would have liked to continue, but I stopped. Out of respect I stopped and rearranged the pillow. Moving away from the bed, before leaving the room, I made the sign of the cross. The mystery was veiled—a great mystery made up of small, humble things.

Only when I was out in the corridor and turned my attention to the voices rising from the bottom of the stair-case did I realize that I wore the same smile on my face as the Asian nun and the young woman had after leaving their notes in the room.

I

Bakhita: The Miraculous Black Woman

The room truly exists—as it existed for the one who just wrote about it. The room with the young woman and the nun, their smiles and their handwritten notes. It is the room where Bakhita slept and where she died. Bakhita, the first saint from Sudan, was an African woman who was beaten and tortured as the slave of a powerful Arab merchant and of a Turkish general. Ransomed in Khartoum at the end of the nineteenth century by the Italian vice-consul and brought to Venice, she worked as the family nursemaid and was baptized. She joined the Canossian Daughters of Charity founded by Saint Magdalene of Canossa and became a saint, living for fifty years in the convent on Via Fusinato in the town of Schio, in the Italian province of Vicenza.

Kidnapped as a child by slave traders, Bakhita was bought and sold five times over, as are many children in Africa and across the globe even to this day. Of her family Bakhita remembered nothing. She did not remember the name her father and mother gave her. She remembered only the Arab nickname the slave traders gave her as a sort of backhanded compliment: Bakhita, that is, "Lucky".

She did not even remember her own language, because her masters forced her to speak Arabic. When she came to Italy, she did not learn Italian but rather the dialect spoken in the Veneto region in northeastern Italy—or, more accurately, a mixture of *vicentino* (a variant of the Veneto dialect spoken in and around the province of Vicenza), *veneziano* (the dialect of Venice), and Italian, cobbled together in such a way that it sometimes sounded eccentric yet was always extremely effective in conveying wisecracks and idiomatic expressions.

African as a person from Sudan, Italian as a person living in Italy, Bakhita, like so many country women of that era in the Po River valley, barely knew how to read and could not write. She was poor, but her poverty was freely chosen. She was so poor that after her death, the only items found inside the one drawer in her room were a little crucifix, a rosary, and a small prayer book. She patched her clothes so many times that they were held together completely by darning thread. Her humble weather-beaten shoes are on display today in the tiny museum dedicated to her at the Canossian convent in Schio.

After spending several years in Italy in the service of a family from Mirano Veneto (outside Venice), Bakhita was welcomed by the Canossian Sisters as a catechumen and then later as a novice. They taught her how to read a little, but she never really learned how to write.

Those who learned the most, however, were those who lived near her and those who at a certain point began seeking her out, relying on her, asking for her support and, especially, for her prayers. They learned about humility, total poverty, serenity, courtesy, and joyfulness from a broad smile that lit up her black face like a revelation. And they learned what it meant to have an intense desire to be in dialogue with God—the *Paròn*, as she called him in the Venetan dialect.

The *Paròn* is the Master whom one obeys with alacrity, yet not out of obligation or through coercion but because "obedience is pleasing to the Lord." When Bakhita was a slave, she was forced to obey, or else she was whipped. After she became a Christian, she gladly obeyed the Lord. She said, "When I am with him wherever he wants me to be, I feel so good inside and out: he is the Master, and I am his poor little creature." The Lord is a good Master who never deserts his servants, who guides and accompanies them in every moment of their lives. "I give everything to the *Paròn*, and he takes care of me—he is obliged to." He is a demanding yet loving Master, ready to make up for what is lacking in the one who serves him with love. Thus, to a somewhat superficial person who was amazed at how Bakhita always succeeded in doing God's will with joy and without showing weariness, she responded, "Do you think it is easy to please the *Paròn*? Nevertheless, I do all that I can. He does the rest."

And she prayed, hour after hour in front of the tabernacle, before the crucifix. She prayed, content to be in the presence of her Lord, simply meditating on his life so as "to learn how to love him better". She prayed unceasingly, for, says the Curé of Ars—another great saint of humility and prayer, who was in love with God to the point of exhaustion—"the more you pray, the more you desire to pray. It is like a fish that first swims in shallow waters and then starts going out deeper and deeper. Our souls are the same: once engulfed in the depths, the soul loses itself in the sweetness of the conversation with God."

The *Paròn* is faithful, in life as in death. And when he decided that the time had come for Bakhita to return to him, she understood and was content. As she explained to a person who asked whether she was afraid of death, "When someone is so in love with another, all that person desires is to be close to him. So why should I be so afraid of death? Death brings us to God."

We have a great deal of evidence that confirms these affirmations. Through her sufferings and death, Bakhita has helped multiply, as it were, the grace God pours out upon the world—intercessions of every kind, conversions, healings, resolutions of family feuds and heartaches. This grace is a mysterious and endless trail of love, of forgiveness and spiritual fruitfulness, the source of a desire for dialogue and reconciliation that spans the globe and that is bearing much fruit above all in Africa.

"If the Lord allows it," she affirmed repeatedly in the weeks and days before her death, "I will send so many graces from paradise for the salvation of souls." This is the logical consequence of a life given over entirely to the love of God for the sake of bringing God's creatures back to him. Thus, when the illness no longer allowed her prayers to be accompanied as usual by actions, her principal task became that of interceding for sinners and those who suffer. At this point, incapable of movement, Bakhita declared, "Now my mission is this: to help everyone by way of prayer."

The notes left under her pillow are not the only sign that many find Bakhita a sure source of spiritual aid. The number of people around the world who offer testimony about their answered prayers through Bakhita's intercession grows daily. Similarly, year after year, devotion to Saint Bakhita continues to spread. The number of parents who name their daughters Bakhita is also increasing, not only in Africa, Asia, and South America but also in Europe, in Italy.

Among Italians, a good number of people can still say that they knew Bakhita. Many remember hearing the stories she would tell them in her husky voice, stories about her life as a ransomed slave. Others recall being struck by her irresistible smile, by her gentleness, and by how she always made herself available to others. And then there are those who have been touched spiritually or physically through her prayers, as well as others whose prayer lives have been reignited after discovering her through one of the tens of thousands of copies of books that recount her life story.

That Bakhita was a black woman much loved by white people might at first seem unremarkable. But as a refugee in the nineteenth century who lived through the first half of the twentieth, Bakhita witnessed an age when racism produced horrors. She is then a special reference point for any and all who suffer discrimination.

The initiatives that seek to honor Bakhita are constantly growing. Numerous chapels, prayer groups, parishes, vocation centers, hospitals, schools, welcome centers, social and cultural centers, and even religious communities and congregations are dedicated to her. These kinds of developments are taking place all around the world, particularly in Africa, South America, and Italy.

Wherever devotion to this saint springs up, it spreads by way of the mysterious paths of poverty, spontaneity, and humility. In places where Bakhita was nowhere to be found, now she is there. And then you realize that perhaps she was already there to begin with. It was a matter of simply taking a closer look around, having a little more humility to notice her image on the hospital bedside table or a copy of her biography among the few books leaning side by side in a poor person's home.

In so many of these places Bakhita's arrival has gone unnoticed, but she has always come through the front door, even if by accident, thanks to a friend, a Canossian sister, a miraculously led person, a simple admirer, a Comboni missionary, an African, a Sudanese refugee, or one of Opus Dei's 250,000 members who could be found in Saint Peter's Square on the day when both Saints Josemaría Escrivà and Bakhita were beatified. If the miracles and answered prayers that have taken place through Bakhita's intercession follow the pathway of the Holy Spirit, then her popularity and her smile follow the most spontaneous pathway of all—word of mouth.

One of the striking things about Bakhita—who actually met a saint like Pius X (who thought very highly of her and whom she admired as well)—is that she has developed an extraordinary spiritual relationship with saints such as Escrivá and Daniel Comboni, neither of whom she ever met, based on the shared mission of spreading the love of Christ. And then there is the mother-daughter relationship that unites her with Magdalene of Canossa, the holy foundress of the Canossians, with whom she shared a deep devotion to Christ Crucified and to the Eucharist as well a passion for prayer and humility. This passion is palpable evidence pointing directly to the path of Christ. "At one time, when I was young," writes Augustine in his *Sermons*, "I read Sacred Scripture rather as a means of cultivating sharp arguments rather than as a source of spiritual wisdom. With this self-serving attitude I myself closed the door on the Lord. Instead of knocking loudly so that he might open it, I closed myself up. In my pride I dared to seek what can be found only with humility."

Particularly struck by Bakhita's huge impact on people are the Comboni missionaries who work throughout Africa, especially among those who live in the difficult environment of Sudan. They are struck because Bakhita is considered more than just a saint in Sudan. She is a promise of freedom, a sign of Africa's redemption. She is proof that God does not abandon his people. She is a palpable point of reference for the Catholic communities and for the local Church, which is forced to submit to daily discrimination and abuse (often to the point of martyrdom) in a country ruled by Islamic law—where, as soon as one travels outside the major cities, non-Muslim children can be abducted and forced into slavery as they were in Bakhita's time, because the only law that counts is the man who is stronger.[1] Bakhita is our "universal sister", as Pope John Paul II dubbed her on the day he raised her to the glory of the altars. The Canossian theologian Father Amedeo Cencini speaks of her as "the most attractive of saints". Indeed, her popularity is staggering and continues to reach new countries, new villages, new cities. The Canossians themselves, who have missions worldwide, are amazed to find Bakhita and her miracles in places where they had not yet even thought about starting a mission.

---

[1] It should be noted that the political landscape in Sudan has changed dramatically since the publication of the Italian edition of this book in 2000. In 2005 the twenty-two-year civil war in Sudan ended, and on July 9, 2011, South Sudan became an independent democratic state, not ruled by Islamic law.— TRANS.

II

Childhood in Africa

The sources

"The Lord has always been good to me my whole life." "The Lord has always watched over me." "My entire life has been a gift of God." These are some of the responses Bakhita gave to those who asked her about her life story. This was not a lack of willingness on her part but rather humility, a sense of modesty and discretion, and the desire to give credit to God above all else.

Many recalled how Mother Josephine Bakhita often gave them the gift (everyone who listened to her called it a "gift") of recounting an episode from her life in Africa. It was above all to children that she preferred telling these stories. The little lodgers in the Canossian house in Schio often asked the black sister for a story. Instead of telling them fairy tales, Bakhita talked about how as a little girl she was kidnapped and became a slave.

It was hard for her to tell these stories, however. She felt uncomfortable putting her suffering on display. She was shy about confiding these things, even to the sisters of her own religious order during her travels to cities and towns in northern Italy, in the Marches region, and in Tuscany, promoting the missions. She felt too much like an object of curiosity. "They want to see a beautiful beast", she said, possibly reliving the humiliations she suffered at the slave markets.

It hurt to tell her story, but she did so nonetheless. "For the glory of God, to exalt the power of God, who showed me his salvation"—this is how she almost always began her stories. Then her humility eventually yielded to the joy of giving voice to experiences that she knew were guided by the hand of God.

No written records remain of these stories that she told in countless piazzas and parish halls. What do remain are the memories of those who listened to them, such as Father Gabriele Amorth, the exorcist, who as a boy in Modena went with all his classmates one day to hear all about the black nun. What sticks in his memory is how impressed he was by Bakhita's joviality, her exuberance, and her extraordinarily communicative personality.

In addition to the direct testimonies of those who knew her personally (and even some of these testimonies are based on hearsay or accounts found in biographies), there are three possible roads one can take for discovering the true story about Bakhita's early years. The first is a manuscript dictated by Mother Josephine to a Canossian sister in 1910 at the request of her superior at the time, Mother Margherita Bonotto. This thirty-five-page autobiography, shorn of some historical imprecisions and observations (and words) that clearly derive from the Italian experience of both the one dictating and the one writing, should be considered the primary source of information covering the period from Bakhita's childhood until her arrival in Italy.

The second and much more well-known source is the biography written by Ida Zanolini.[1] She first encountered

---

[1] The first edition of Zanolini's book, *Storia meravigliosa* (*Tale of Wonder*), appeared in 1931. Two updated and expanded editions were published later

Bakhita in Venice in 1929 (they met again in 1935), and the book is based on their extensive conversations together. This is certainly a reliable source, yet the literary style and certain emphases clearly reflect the era in which it was written.

The third source consists of the voluminous evidence gathered for the causes of her beatification and canonization. This documentation obviously has a different intent from that of a biography.

There may yet exist a fourth source, although it could be irretrievably lost. Another dictated biography, also from 1929, was written in Schio by Sister Mariannina Turco at the express request of Bakhita herself, who wanted to present it as a gift to the children and grandchildren of Illuminato Checchini, a pivotal figure in her life, as we shall soon discover. In reality, all we actually know about this manuscript, compiled in the fall of that year, comes from what Sister Turco reported about it:

> One day she asked me to write down what she wanted to dictate to me about some of her childhood memories.... I willingly agreed to her request and with the permission of our mother superior, during the free time outside of school hours, I acted as her secretary. At the time, *Storia meravigliosa* (*Tale of Wonder*) had not yet appeared; nobody even thought it would. She sketched out the general outline of the events of her painful story as a slave, all the while marveling at the mysterious way of providence in guiding the events in that little girl's life to such a surprising and supernatural end. I became in a certain way her

---

by the same author. Translated into all European languages, the book has sold hundreds of thousands of copies.

confidante, and she often repeated to me, also at my request, many memories that she preserved from her childhood and of the way of life in her country. Every time I asked her a question about these things, she would respond with such admirable kindness.

In telling the story of Bakhita's life from her childhood to her religious vows in 1896, we will therefore rely on the text of the 1910 autobiography, which in the pages that follow will appear in italics. The paragraphs that flesh out the historical context and numerous details (including certain corrections) as well as the more extensive commentary are all clearly distinguished by the nonitalicized typeface.

With the spirit of Bakhita

In order to begin reading this story with the right spirit—or, better yet, with the spirit of Bakhita—it is important to know what she herself thought about all that had been written and was being written about her life. Responding to one of the many questions posed by a person who was amazed by the extraordinary events he had read about her life—in the course of which he asked whether it all corresponded to the truth—Bakhita answered, "Regarding the truth, it is rather less than more. Because so many true things have been seen by the Lord alone, they cannot be spoken about or written down."

These words help us to understand both the humility and the Christological lens through which the Sudanese nun interpreted her life, convinced that God's hand guided it from the very first moment of her existence. These are words

33

that at the same time suggest that we are still unaware of the full extent of Bakhita's suffering as well as the full depths of Bakhita's spirituality.

Besides, as we will learn shortly, there are two episodes in the Sudanese saint's life that she revealed in strict confidence only at the end of her life. Not surprisingly, these are episodes that consist precisely in what is most painful and humiliating and that will have the greatest spiritual and mystical impact among the many who know about them.

There is also another topic of which we should be well aware while reading. Bakhita never viewed the sufferings she endured as a mark of merit. If anything, in her great simplicity, she considered the notoriety that came to her through Zanolini's book a great suffering. Because she was humble and sought to live in union and in dialogue with God as much as possible, Bakhita tended to shy away from anything that could distract her from her principal mission.

In 1955 the forty-four-year-old Giovanna Santulin, who attended the Canossian high school in Schio during the 1920s and provided testimony for the diocesan beatification process, recalled very well the day when "it was my turn to clean the church and I saw that the Little Brown Mother[2] had torn up a handwritten notebook containing memories of her life. I asked why, and she answered that she did not want others to know about her sufferings."

This incident not only offers us the criterion for a respectful meditation on Bakhita's life but also increases the likelihood that parts of the Sudanese saint's life will always remain a mystery.

---

[2] *Madre Moretta* (Little Brown Mother): this is the term of endearment by which she was affectionately known in Schio.

My family

By the wish of Reverend Mother Superior, I here dictate some of the events in my life when I was a slave. May these recollections of mine serve to make me always better appreciate the great gift God has given to me in choosing me to be his spouse.

My family lived in the very center of Africa, in a village of the Darfur region called Olgossa, near Mount Agilerei. I was raised by my father and my mother, with three brothers, three sisters, and four others I never knew because they died before I was born. I had a twin sister, whom, like the rest of my family, I never saw again after I was kidnapped. Up until then I had had a very happy life, never knowing what it meant to suffer.

One day my mother decided to go out into the fields, where we had many crops and livestock, to see if the workers were doing their jobs, and she wanted all of us children to go with her. My oldest sister did not want to go, and she asked to stay at home and was allowed to do so with my youngest sister.[3]

While we were in the fields, we suddenly heard a big commotion, with lots of yelling and running. Each of us immediately imagined that the slave traders had come to plunder our village. We quickly returned home, and to our dismay we were told by the little one, all frightened and trembling, how the marauders had carried the older sister away and how she herself had only just barely escaped by hiding behind the wall of a broken-down house; otherwise she would have been kidnapped as well. I still remember how much my mother wept and how much we cried too.

That evening, when my father returned from work, he was told what had happened. Enraged, he immediately set out with his workers in search for her everywhere. But it was in vain. Nothing

[3] Bakhita's twin.

*more is known about my poor sister. This was my first experience
of suffering, and oh, how many more would soon follow.*

Historical references and social realities

Based on the historical and geographical references con-
cerning the events of Bakhita's early life, as well as her appar-
ent age when she arrived in Italy, it can be affirmed that
she was born in 1869, the year the Suez Canal was opened.
Some historical indications suggest that her birth year could
have been 1868 or 1867 but no earlier.

Bakhita's family lived in the village of Olgossa (a mis-
spelling of the Arabic word *Al-Goz* or *Al-Qoz*, meaning
"sandy hill") in the Darfur region. Today the town is vaguely
identifiable. It is situated in Sudan, southwest of the capital
city of Khartoum, about twelve miles from the present city
of Nyala (which in the Daju language literally means "Let's
go chat"), in southern Darfur, near the border with Chad.
This is a vast area dominated by the Jebel Marra mountain
range, with peaks rising to ten thousand feet. Within this
region are the Daju mountains (or hills, really), among which
stands Mount Agilerei (1640 feet), which Bakhita mentions.

Daju is also the name of the native people to which Bakhita belonged. It is one of the many tribes that live in that
part of Africa today. Beginning in the seventeenth century,
this entire area was controlled by the For tribe, whom the
Arabs called the Fur and from which the whole area takes
its name: Darfur, "home of the Fur". Curiously, Mother
Josephine notes that she came from the center of Africa,
and in fact, measuring according to latitude, we find that
the Red Sea to the east and the Atlantic Ocean to the west
are both two thousand miles away from Bakhita's hometown.

The climate of Darfur varies a great deal, from a Saharan environment in the north to a more temperate zone in the south, which benefits from the Jebel Marra mountains, as they collect water and distribute it through springs and streams. A rocky savannah spreads out to the east. The lands of the Daju tribe, which were much greener in Bakhita's day, consist of fertile zones interspersed with drier and sandier areas that resemble the savannah. Today this land is largely populated by seminomadic herdsmen.

The Daju, whose skin is very black, live in the hills of the same name as well as in the borderland straddling Chad and in Kordofan, which is the vast region of southern and central Sudan.

From the accounts of those who heard Mother Josephine tell her story more than once, we know that she belonged to a well-to-do family. Her uncle was the village chief, and her parents cultivated grain on several local farms. Speaking about her parents, Bakhita affirms more than once how good they were. Her father was monogamous and, like his brothers, was raised to respect his fellowman and the things of nature.

The kidnapping

I was around nine years old[4] when one morning, after breakfast, I went with one of my friends, who was eleven or twelve years old, on a walk in our fields, away from the house. Having finished our games, we decided to go pick some herbs.

[4] We need to keep in mind that in an African village in the 1800s, no one, let alone a child, knew how to calculate his own age. The most recent reconstructions of Bakhita's life nonetheless hold that she could not have been more than eight or nine years old.

All of a sudden we saw two armed strangers come out from behind a hedge. They approached us, and one of them said to my friend, "Let this little one go over there by the woods to pick up a bundle for me. She'll be right back. You continue on down the road, and she'll meet up with you soon."

Their plan was to separate me from my friend, because if she were present when they captured me, she would have sounded the alarm. I did not suspect anything. I quickly went and obeyed, as I always did with my mother.

As soon as I entered the woods, looking for the bundle that I could not find, I realized that those two were right behind me. One grabbed me roughly with one hand while he pulled out a big knife from his belt with the other. He put the point of the knife against my side and with a demanding voice said, "If you scream, you're dead. Now move it. Follow us." The other one pushed me, aiming the barrel of his gun at my back. I was petrified. With eyes wide-open and trembling from head to toe, I tried to yell, but a lump in my throat prevented me. I was unable to speak or cry.

Violently pushed through the thick woods, along hidden pathways and over fields, I was made to walk at a fast pace until evening. I was dead tired. My feet and legs were bleeding from stepping on sharp rocks and from walking through thorny brambles. All I could do the whole time was sob, but those hard hearts felt no pity.

Finally, passing through a field of watermelons,[5] which were very plentiful in that area, we halted for a rest. They gathered a few melons and handed me a piece to eat. But I could not swallow any, though I had not eaten since morning. All I could think about was my family. I called for my mommy and daddy with indescribable

[5] This reference to watermelons leads us to believe that the kidnapping took place between February and March (probably in the year 1878), the season in which this fruit grows in great abundance in the wild in the vast plains of central Sudan, between Darfur and Kordofan.

38

anguish. But nobody could hear me there. What was worse, those two ordered me to be quiet with terrible threats. So, tired and on an empty stomach, I was forced to continue the journey on foot through the whole night.

At dawn we arrived in their village. I could not have gone any farther. One of the men grasped me by the hand and dragged me to his home and put me in a storage room full of tools and scraps of wood. There was no bed or covering of any kind. The bare earth would have to serve as both. I was given a piece of dark bread and was told, "Stay here." Then the door was closed and locked with a key.

Bakhita, the "lucky one"

At this point in Mother Josephine's story we need to take a brief look at Ida Zanolini's retelling of these events twenty years after they took place. Her interview with the Sudanese nun reveals the origin and meaning of the name Bakhita, and Zanolini reconstructs the episode in her book in the following way:

It was nightfall when we came out of the woods, but the two Arabs did not show signs of slowing down ... "Black girl, what is your name?" asked the one who kept hold of her ... The little one ... wanted to reply but could not ... "Answer!" ordered the slave driver, rudely ... A few incoherent syllables spilled from her lips ... "Call her Bakhita, and don't waste your time with that little snot-nose", said the other with a crack of his whip ... "Do you understand? From now on your name is Bakhita. And don't forget it." What an ironic name! Bakhita means "lucky", and in that moment who could be more unlucky than she?

Her real name, therefore, was not Bakhita but rather a name in the Daju language. Even had the kidnappers known her real name, it is likely that they would have changed it. With the name Bakhita they probably hoped to begin the process of Arabization and Islamization that was customarily imposed on slave children. It was not by chance that they used a very common Arab name. Bakhita comes from the masculine word *Bakhit*, and, as Zanolini correctly explains, in Arabic it means "lucky". That there was an ironic or even malicious intent in the choice of such a name cannot be excluded. What is certain is that from then on, bearing an Arabic name, Bakhita began a journey that would lead her to be known throughout the world as a Christian saint. Fifteen years later she was baptized with that name. In 1992, after nearly 120 years, the name Bakhita would be enrolled for the first time in the roster of Catholic saints, becoming a sign of God's intimacy and a symbol of freedom and hope for many Catholics in Sudan and throughout the world who experience religious repression on a daily basis, even to the point of martyrdom.

The happiness of the origins

We resume the story where we left off, in a sort of utility closet where Bakhita had been locked by her kidnappers.

I was kept there for over a month. A little hole in the ceiling was my window. The door was opened only momentarily to give me a little bit of food. How much I suffered in that place cannot be put into words. I still remember those hours of anguish when, exhausted from crying, I would fall to the floor, limp, completely numb, while my imagination carried me to my loved ones far, far away.

There, I saw my parents, brothers, and sisters, and I hugged them all with joy and tenderness, telling them how I'd been kidnapped and how much I had suffered. Other times I would be playing with my friends in our fields, and I felt happy. But alas, when I returned to the hard reality of my horrible solitude, I was overcome by a feeling of discouragement that seemed to shatter my heart.

These last words testify to Bakhita's great human sensitivity. After more than forty years, including fifteen years of religious life, she describes the pain and sentiments she felt as a young girl as if she had experienced them only yesterday, with a naturalness and simplicity that is astounding. What consistently emerges in her stories and even informal exchanges is that Africa remained ever close to her heart, just like her family and the happiness of her earliest years (which she relived in her dreams). It is a happiness that for Bakhita was surpassed only by the supreme joy of the encounter with God, which is the obvious sign of the futility of so many of our contemporary secular approaches to understanding and aspiring to happiness in life. Herein lies an implicit critique (regardless of whether Mother Bakhita was aware of it or not) of the methods by which Europe has for so long sought to impose an economic and cultural logic, with all its contradictions, upon peoples in principle considered to be uncivilized, in spite of the obvious diversity from region to region, ethnic group to ethnic group, and tribe to tribe.

The slave trade in Africa: Yesterday

Beginning in the seventeenth century, Africa became the principal area for supplying slaves to the colonies in the West Indies. As a result, the continent was split in two. The

Atlantic side of Africa, from Senegal to Angola, became the hunting ground for slaves destined to work on the American and European plantations in the New World and, later, also in the African colonies. The eastern side, which comprises the Horn of Africa, including Sudan and Chad and the neighboring regions to the west as far as the high valley of the Niger River, was in the hands of the Arab slave trade, which exported to the Middle East (the Arabian Peninsula) and served the houses of the rich Muslim North Africans, Turks, and Egyptians who lived in Tunisia, Libya, Egypt, and the Nile River valley as far as the city of Khartoum, founded by the pasha Muhammad Ali (governor of Egypt under the sultan of Istanbul) between 1821 and 1822.

In 1821 Muhammad Ali sent two armies to conquer Sudan. The political objective was to establish a dynasty of his own in the region, but the practical objectives were to plunder wealth[6] and to capture slaves for his personal army. Thus, the year 1821 witnessed the beginning of what would amount to six decades of Turkish-Egyptian rule over Sudan. Darfur, however, which was an independent sultanate, was conquered only in 1875.

The caravan routes became the favored thoroughfares for the slave trade—from the interior of Africa to the ports of the Red Sea and the Mediterranean, from the island of Zanzibar to the trading posts with European merchants and African tribes that provided slaves from the eastern coast. The slave trade was a flourishing business, around which, at a certain point in time, the entire Ottoman and Islamic economy turned. When the British banned the slave trade in the second half of the nineteenth century, it was not by accident that commerce came to a standstill and the entire

[6] Travelers in this era report the presence of gold in the rivers and in mines.

Nile region fell under British control. In opposition to this ban and subsequent British supremacy, the fundamentalist revolution of the Mahdi erupted in 1881—a revolution that would play a key role in Bakhita's arrival in Italy.

On the threshold of the twentieth century, however, the selling of black Africans did not cease.[7] Nevertheless, during the first half of the nineteenth century, nearly all of the great European powers and the United States enacted laws decreeing the end of the slave trade and of slavery. The first country that formally abolished slavery was France in 1794, but in 1802 Napoleon reintroduced it. In 1807 the British government prohibited the slave trade between Africa and America. In 1827, thirty-eight years after the War of Independence, the state of New York outlawed slavery. With the Abolition Act of 1833, Great Britain prohibited every form of slavery while explicitly excluding its colonies in the East from this ban. Between 1834 and 1849 Great Britain, France, and Holland, in that order, forbade the use of slaves on their sugar cane plantations in the Caribbean. This decision, however, coincided with the increased cultivation of beets in Europe. In Africa the Germans prohibited (though only formally) the sale of slaves in 1895. The Italians forbade it in Somalia in 1903.

---

[7] In the hope of limiting the slave trade, in 1890 the French cardinal from Algiers, Charles Martial Lavigerie, founded a unique military-religious community, the Frères armés du Sahara (Armed brothers of the Sahara). It was an order of soldier-monks whose primary goal was to counter the slave trade in the caravans of east central Africa, creating outposts where they gave safe haven to escaped or freed slaves, welcomed travelers, and tilled the land as an example for the local population. It was an enterprise that lasted only a couple of years. Lavigerie himself, after 1870, as a missionary in the Great Lakes region of eastern Africa, successfully used numerous papal Zouaves who were out of work after the breach of Porta Pia in order to protect his mission-farm villages from Arab slave traders.

In reality, up until the first decades of the twentieth century, the formal bans on the slave trade were systematically circumvented by the Europeans and also, through duplicitous decisions, by Western powers in defense of their immediate interests.[8] In the colonies, the slaves were replaced by imported workers who were given forced contracts or who were taken on as unpaid apprentices—Africans first, then Indians and Chinese. At the same time, laws against vagrancy (in Nigeria and Mozambique) affected unemployed ex-slaves. In many cases, these ex-slaves were forcibly recruited by the occupying armies.

In order to grasp this ambiguous state of affairs more fully and to see how Western nations continued to exchange human beings for economic gain despite the bans and legal regulations, it is worth reporting several incidents involving colonial New England and then the United States.

At the end of the 1600s, the English colonies on the east coast of America began to acquire economic and commercial power by practicing three-way or four-way commerce. From Boston and other northern ports, ships set sail for western Africa, where they exchanged rum and low-quality salted cod for loads of slaves that were then traded in the Caribbean for sugar and molasses, which were in turn sold in North America, where rum was produced with

[8] The English, French, and Portuguese employed a juridical tactic with the twofold goal of economic gain and of silencing the ever-growing antislavery movements in Europe. They transformed large portions of their overseas territories into protectorates (which, unlike colonies, did not directly depend upon the central governments). This legal arrangement offered economic benefits as well as easier relationships with local authorities, since it tolerated the exploitation of the indigenous population by means that included slavery. In these regions, European citizens were even allowed to own slaves. In Mauritania, for example, the French concessions to the slave-trading indigenous tribes produced a sort of legalization of slavery that is still in effect today.

the molasses. From the same ports, hundreds of ships loaded with salted cod that had been fished off Newfoundland set out each year bound for the French, English, and Dutch Caribbean islands, where, beginning in the 1700s, it was discovered that the most economical way to maintain slaves on the plantations was to feed them cod.

And yet we are talking about the American colonies, whose Declaration of Independence of 1776 states that "all men are created equal." [9] Slavery nevertheless persisted into the nineteenth century, so that in 1835 the practice was reported by the French thinker Alexis de Tocqueville in *Democracy in America*, which details his visit to the United States. And such is the contradiction that even in 1936, Felton and Company—the rum works founded in Boston in the early 1800s—in advertising its products as the fruit of an ancient tradition, candidly published the following line: "The shipping owners developed a cycle of exchange that included cargoes of slaves bound for the West Indies, cargoes of fine molasses from those islands bound for Boston and other ports in New England, and finally shipments of rum bound for Africa."

The slave trade in Africa: Today

Bakhita, and her sister before her, were abducted between 1875 and 1878 by nomadic Arab shepherds from Kordofan called Baggara. The Baggara kidnapped children and young

[9] The author of the Declaration of Independence, Thomas Jefferson, was a slave owner. John Adams, another of the founding fathers of the American nation, refused, on principle, to use slave labor, defining the practice as "cruel war against human nature". Nevertheless, he defended the cod and molasses trade with the English, French, and Dutch territories in the Caribbean, even though such business transactions depended directly upon slavery.

women (who sold for more than men) for the markets to the north and east. Before 1875 the Darfur region, as an independent sultanate, was off limits to the northern merchants. Its annexation to the Ottoman Empire came as a result, strangely enough, of the activity of the private army (made up of five hundred slaves) of a powerful Arab slave trader originally from Bahr el Ghazal, a man by the name of Zubeir Mansur Rahma.

In those regions, kidnappings and abductions of non-Muslim black Africans (above all, young women and children) continued with minor fluctuations through the 1900s at the hands of Muslim African tribes and various irregular armies. A good number of the slaves were exported (some scholars and missionaries claim that the verb should still be used in the present tense) to the Arabian Peninsula (Saudi Arabia formally abolished slavery only in 1960, and Oman ten years later). The remainder (today almost the entirety) were traded internally. In Ethiopia, for example, slavery was an institution until the 1960s.

One hundred and thirty years later, at the beginning of a new millennium, Bakhita's story reads like today's daily news. In present-day Africa, there still exist zones (like Bahr el Ghazal in Sudan, and the north of Uganda) or states, like Mauritania, where the exploitation of slaves (abducted in the less accessible parts or from equatorial Africa) takes place in the light of day and according to ancient custom. This has been proved by systematic reports from Amnesty International and Anti-Slavery International. In the Sudanese markets of Safaha, El Dhein, Kadogli, and Awiel, a black slave can cost $100 or more, but in many cases also much less. "In Sudan," explains Claudio Monici, correspondent for the daily newspaper *Avvenire* and an expert on Africa, "the Khartoum government's continuous denials notwithstanding, slavery is a given fact." On several occasions in *Avvenire*, Monici has reported stories of dozens of African slaves in our times. These slaves include Mohammed Ibrahim, a Dinka who was kidnapped so young that when he was freed at the age of thirteen he did not know a single word from his native language but spoke only Arabic; Ayak Deng, a Dinka girl kidnapped to be used as an "impregnation animal" to produce other slaves; and John, a young Acholi abducted by guerilla warriors from the Lord's Resistance Army in the north of Uganda, taken to southern Sudan and transformed into a child slave and soldier. He told the story himself: "They came to my village at night and destroyed all the homes. I was captured along with a dozen others my age ... The three girls from our group were soon forced to prostitute themselves with the leaders ... When we went into combat, there was only one order: to kill. To kill our people."

In Bakhita's time, in the Nile valley and in the Horn of Africa, the preferred hunting ground of the slave traders was Darfur, Kordofan, and Chad in the west and southern Ethiopia and Somalia in the east. Today it is the animist and Christian populations of southern Sudan, northern Kenya, and Uganda who are the objects of child-kidnapping raids. These children are then used as fodder by the various guerilla armies that operate in the area, or else they are sold to rich landowners in the north (it is said as far as southern Libya), though precise data do not exist in the latter case. It is known that little children are abducted and are taught Arabic so that as soon as possible they forget their origins.

This is essentially what happened to Bakhita. And to show how relevant the story of the Sudanese saint is today, it is worth quoting in full the vivid admonition that parents in Bahr el Ghazal, where the Dinka population lives, have been transmitting orally to their children for generations:

47

They will put a collar around your neck and chains around your ankles. Son, you will no longer feel the wind of the savannah, the freedom of your people. At the market they will touch you to see how strong you'll be for work. A man will pay to buy you like a sack of coal to be thrown in the fire. Daughter, they will also steal your womb from you. Remember, children, you must always wake up early, even before dawn. Be ready to escape into the woods when the Arabs arrive on their horses whose mouths foam with rage. You will not hear the voices of your parents anymore, whose throats will have been slit, but rather the tinkling of iron that will accompany you in your life as a slave.

Monsignor Cesare Mazzolari, bishop of Rumbek in southern Sudan, in an interview with *Avvenire* on December 24, 1999, confirmed this bleak reality: "This people lives in constant danger. They live in fear that at night a group of Arabs will arrive on horseback, the Morahilin, to plunder everything, to kidnap, and to kill." [10]

This brings to mind the lament of Daniel Comboni, [11] who in 1873 (several years before Bakhita was kidnapped) wrote from El Obeid (a key Sudanese city in our story) to a priest friend from Trent: "The Islamic government, which

[10] Father Giulio Albanese, a missionary and journalist who has traveled many times to South Sudan, in 1992 gathered direct testimonies that reveal the following facts: "After being captured, the boys leave for the north, to the slave market of Safara in Darfur, where they are auctioned off ... In Sumeih, the purchase of slaves is done through the train windows: the merchandise is tossed to the ground in front of the highest bidders, who then put the slaves to use as laborers in the fields and as domestic servants and turn the girls (often just children) into concubines. The price for a boy is ten to one hundred dollars. Six boys can be acquired for the price of a light machine gun."

[11] Saint Daniel Comboni, one of the great missionaries in the Church's history, was the founder of two missionary institutes known widely as the Comboni Missionaries and the Comboni Missionary Sisters. He was canonized by Pope John Paul II on October 5, 2003.—TRANS.

complied with the treaty of 1856, complies on paper only, so that slavery is still in full force and the cry of suffering of these peoples does not reach Europe ... Thus the misery in these regions continues apace, and will continue for a long time."

At the slave market

Let us resume the story of Mother Josephine. We had left her in the hands of the kidnappers, who held her in a narrow prison room, waiting to sell her to a slave trader.

One morning my door was opened earlier than usual. The owner presented me to a slave trader, who bought me and put me with his other slaves. They were three men and three women; one was a girl a little older than I.

Soon we were on the road. Just seeing the countryside, the sky, the water, just being able to breathe fresh air gave me a bit of life again, even though I did not know where I would end up. The journey lasted eight straight days—always on foot through woods, over hills, through valleys and deserts.

This is how the caravan was arranged: first the men, then the women. Everyone had a thick chain fastened around his neck, locked with a key and padlock, connecting two or three in a row. Woe to anyone who bent over or stopped—the poor necks of that person and his companion. You could see big, deep wounds around all the necks. It was so pitiful.

They strapped big loads onto the backs of the strongest men, who then had to carry them for miles and miles. Those poor men, how they were turned into beasts of burden. We little ones did not have chains. We walked at the end of the line with the owners. We stopped only for a few hours to rest and have some food. Then the chain was removed from around the neck and fastened to the feet, one step away from the next person, so as to prevent anyone from running away. This was also done to us little ones, but only at night.

Finally we reached the slave market. We were brought into a big room to await our turn to be sold. The weakest and sickly were the first to be sold off, for fear that if they got worse the traders would lose their profits. Poor victims!

The two of us who were the smallest were always close to one another, since our feet were tied together by the same chain. When nobody was watching, we would tell each other our stories, how we had been kidnapped. We talked about our dear families, and our talk increased our desire to return to our families more and more. As we lamented our unhappy fate, we also thought about plans somehow to escape. The good Lord, who was watching over us—though we did not realize it at the time—gave us such an occasion. Here is how it happened.

Escape and deception

The owner put us in a separate room and always locked us in, especially when he had to leave the house.

It was almost dinnertime. Having returned from the market, he led to the house a mule loaded with ears of corn. He came and undid our chains, ordering us to unload the corn and to feed the mule. He then departed, absentmindedly leaving the door unlocked. We were alone and without chains. God's providence—now was the time.

A glance of mutual agreement, a handshake, a quick look around, and, nobody in sight, we were off as fast as our poor legs could carry us, running toward the open countryside without knowing where we were going. The whole night was one continuous, anxiety-ridden race through the woods and over desert terrain. Panting and out of breath, in the darkness we could hear wild animals growling. When they got close, we saved ourselves by climbing up trees.

One time we had just come down from our shelter and had resumed our footrace when we heard a buzzing sound, typical of approaching caravans. We hid behind bushes bristling with thorns. For a good two hours one group followed after the other right in front of us, but nobody caught sight of us. It was only the good Lord who protected us, no other.

I thought that once these dangers were over I would then quickly be able to find my dear family again. This gave me courage, and I suffered everything willingly for this goal. Alas, who knows how far away from them I traveled instead . . . Toward dawn we halted to catch our breath. How exhausted we were! Our hearts were beating like hammers, our bodies were dripping big beads of sweat, and sharp pangs of hunger pierced our stomachs: we had nothing to eat. The intense desire to be reunited with our families and the fear of being tracked down gave us the strength to continue the race, but not as it had been at the start. Where were we going to end up?

Near sundown we saw a little cottage. Our hearts began to beat rapidly. We strained our eyes to see if it was our house. It was not. What bitterness, how disillusioned we felt! As we stood there thinking about what to do next, a man appeared right in front of us. Frightened, we were about to flee. But he stopped and politely asked us:

"Where are you going?"

We remained silent.

"Come now, tell me: Where are you going?"

"To our parents."

"And where are your parents?"

"Over there", we replied in confusion, pointing vaguely.

He then realized that we were runaways.

"All right then", he said. "Come and have a little rest, and I'll take you to your parents."

Believing his words, we followed him into the cottage. As soon as we were inside, he immediately laid us flat on the ground. He gave us a little water, but we were so worn out that we could not drink it. Then he left us alone for about an hour. After a brief sleep, we were awakened. The man took us to his house, gave us food and drink, and then led us out to a big pen full of goats and sheep. He made some space for an angareb[12] *and then tied our feet together with a big chain, telling us to stay in the pen until we were told what to do next.*

Here we were, slaves again! So much for taking us to our parents. How we cried, how we suffered. We were left there among goats and rams for days, until a slave trader passed through. Then we were taken out of the pen and sold to that man.

We walked a long way before we met up with the caravan. Among the other slaves, we were surprised to discover some who had also belonged to the owner from whom we had just escaped.[13] They described to us the owner's anger and rage once he discovered we were gone. He blamed and beat any slave he happened to see, and he threatened to cut us to pieces when he found us.

I recognize now more than ever the goodness of the Lord, who also miraculously saved me at that time.

We traveled for two and a half weeks,[14] always following the same male-female sequence as before. In one village I was moved to tears to see a poor slave who was in such a bad way that he

[12] A bed of intertwining cords on a wooden frame.

[13] It almost seems that, in spite of her escape, Bakhita was guided along a kind of marked trail.

[14] In order to fathom the barbarous conditions to which the slaves were subject in these caravans, we should point out that on the road between Darfur and El Obeid lies a village called Tawashia. This is an Arabic Sudanese name that means "the geldings". This was a place where certain experts who had gained experience with animals castrated kidnapped children. It was a painful procedure, practiced without even minimal hygiene. Those who survived greatly increased in value and came to be utilized as harem servants.

could not stand up by himself anymore. I begged the owner to let him sit down and rest awhile. He did not believe me and began to beat him like an animal. I saw him fall to the ground, moaning, "I'm going to die. I can't go on." But the inhuman owner hit him even more to make him get up. Seeing that the slave could not move any longer, the owner had to remove the chain that fastened him to his partner. The poor man was whimpering so pitifully that it broke my heart. The owner, now enraged, ordered us to keep going while he stayed there with that unfortunate one. What happened to him? We never saw him again.

The angel

Approximately twenty years after this account was set down in writing, Mother Josephine added something more. Confiding in Sister Mariannina Turco, who was then working on a draft of Bakhita's biography for the Checchinis, Bakhita revealed a detail of great importance that took place during her escape. Sister Turco provided an account of it during the beatification process.

> Bakhita once told me that something happened after she and her companion escaped from their owner, on the very first night they spent in the forest. While everything was dark all around them and they were hiding under some plants, she suddenly saw a beautiful figure take shape in the sky. Surrounded by light, this figure was smiling at her and pointed out the way she should follow. Without telling anything about this to her companion, she confidently followed the direction that this mysterious figure indicated. In this way, she found the strength and courage to continue on, and thus they were saved from the wild beasts. Near dawn the figure disappeared, and she did not see it again.

After many years, when she was a nun and sacristan, without even recalling the earlier occasion in the forest, one morning as she was opening the little door to the rectory,[15] she saw at her side a beautiful young man, radiant with light. Surprised, she stopped, then recognized him and remembered. She wanted to speak but felt as if her tongue had been nailed to the roof of her mouth, and her limbs became all stiff. The young man smiled at her and then disappeared. "It must have been your guardian angel", I told her. "Yes, I believe it was, too", she replied. "But don't tell anyone about this." I promised that I wouldn't.

One day during recreation, we were talking about guardian angels, and I, who was near Bakhita, said to her, "You too, Mother, have seen your guardian angel." She became serious and did not respond. I understood and did not repeat it. After recreation, when we found a moment together, she let me know how I had failed to keep my word and that she would not be pleased were the others to know about that particular incident. I told her I was sorry for being so thoughtless and reassured her that no one had taken notice of the question I asked her, which could be interpreted in a number of ways.

Mother Josephine's need to disclose a new episode about her already-rich childhood experience did not, therefore, arise by chance. Rather, it arose because a short time earlier she had experienced the same extraordinary event, and she wanted to understand, by consulting a sister who was more educated than she, whether her observations about it were plausible.

It is a point of fact that Bakhita liked to talk about guardian angels and many times made specific references to how

[15] This spot can be visited easily at Schio.

her guardian angel was always close by her side. Above all, she spoke about this with children, as Mrs. Aurelia Fuoli remembers perfectly in 1956. Between 1912 and 1913, Mrs. Fuoli was a lodger at the school in Schio: "She often spoke to us about our guardian angel and told us that he was our guide, that we had to follow him and not make him sad."

Mother Josephine, after her second encounter with the angel, fully understood the extraordinary importance of the event, which proved that God had always loved and guided her, even when she did not know he existed. Her sense of spiritual communion reached a level of such naturalness that, in reply to a sister who was overly concerned because the bedridden Bakhita could not go to Mass, she said, "Do not worry. I send my guardian angel so that he will tell me about it later."

The Turkish general

When we finally arrived in the city,[16] *we were brought to the house of the Arab leader.*[17] *He was an extremely rich man and already owned a large number of slaves, all in the flower of their youth. My companion and I were destined to be handmaids of the young ladies who were his daughters, who came to like us. The owner's intention was to present us as gifts to his son when he got married. In that house I was treated well and lacked for nothing.*

[16] This would be El Obeid, capital of Kordofan and at this time the richest and most populated city in Sudan. According to Comboni, who built a mission there, it had over one hundred thousand inhabitants, 80 percent of whom were slaves!

[17] Probably Ilyas Umm Birayr, at the time governor of Kordofan under Gordon Pasha (Charles George Gordon).

Yet one day, I do not know what mistake I made, but it involved the owner's son. He immediately took up his whip to strike me. I fled to the other room in order to hide behind his sisters. I had never done such a thing before! Enraged, he tore me away from there by force and threw me to the ground. With his whip and his feet he gave me many, many blows, and finally, with a kick to my left side, he left me for dead. I do not remember anything after that. I must have been carried by slaves to my bed, where I remained for more than a month. After recovering from the beating, I was assigned to other work. But my time was up. I was to be sent away from that house at the first opportunity.

Such an opportunity came three months later, when I was sold to a new master. He was a general in the Turkish army.[18] With him were his elderly mother and his wife. Both of the women were quite inhumane toward the poor slaves, who were engaged in the most demanding labor in the kitchen, did the laundry, and worked in the fields.

Another young girl and I were at the service of the two ladies. We could not leave their side for a single moment. Between dressing them, cooling them with fans, and perfuming them, we were given no rest. And woe to us if by mistake or out of fatigue we touched even a single hair on the ladies' heads. The blows would fall on us without mercy. In the three years I spent in their service, I do not remember a day going by without my being hit. The wounds I received one day would not be healed before others were added the next, without my knowing why.

One day I told my companion how I had fled my first owner. The general's daughter listened to all of it. Possibly fearing that I would attempt to escape, she made me wear a big chain around my ankles for more than a month. It was taken off on the occasion of

[18] One of the many who had military responsibilities in El Obeid before the Mahdi revolt.

56

a major Muslim holiday,[19] when it was required to remove the shackles from all slaves.

The slaves had to rise every day at dawn. The lady of the house, the general's wife, was so zealous that at times she woke up before everyone to see whether anybody was even a minute late. Then she would be right on top of that person with her whip, making him jump from the pain, without taking into account that the poor soul—and this happened often—had worked late into the night. All the slaves slept in one big room. An absolute fast was in force until midday, when they were given a serving of meat stew, polenta, bread, and fruit. In the evening there was a frugal meal, and then they went to sleep on the floor naked. Woe to anyone who was not quiet. Poor victims of inhuman tyranny.

Those who got sick were not given a single glance but were abandoned. No thought was given to helping them, let alone to offering them medical treatment. When they were about to die, they were thrown out in the fields or on the manure heap.

The poor slaves suffered many abuses and lashings for no reason. For example, one day we happened to be present when the master was arguing with his wife. Just to take it out on someone, he ordered the two of us down to the courtyard and commanded two soldiers to throw us to the ground to be flogged. Those two began this cruel punishment with full force and left both of us covered in blood. I remember how they took aim at my thighs with the cane, taking away skin and flesh and giving me a long gash that left me immobile in bed for months. All of this had to be endured in silence because nobody came to dress our wounds or offer us a word of comfort. How many of my ill-fated companions died from the blows they suffered.

[19] Probably the end of Ramadan.

The Turks set foot in the territory of present-day Sudan in the second decade of the sixteenth century. In 1518 in particular they conquered Nubia, that is, the northern part of the country. Several years prior, Amara Dunqas, the first king of the Funj state (situated in the Nile valley south of Khartoum), was converted to Islam. It was during the course of this century that the traces of Christianity that had existed in the region were progressively erased. This occurred also as a result of the intense importation of Muslim missionaries from the Arabian Peninsula. In the next century, between 1660 and 1680, Sulayman Solong proclaimed Islam the religion of the Darfur state, constructed mosques, and propagated Muslim practices.

The Ottoman presence in the region reached its height beginning in 1821, when a Turco-Egyptian army conquered Sudan south of Nubia, overthrew the Funj state, and founded the city of Khartoum. In the following decades, the Turco-Egyptian administration allowed ample space for the slave trade, and slave traders (the richest and most famous of which was Zubeir Mansour) assumed full control of the hunting grounds in the southern and western parts of the country.

The growing British influence throughout the Nile region—in 1875 Egypt ceded to Great Britain its shareholdings in the Suez Canal—and the resulting imposition of a ban on the slave trade, together with an increase in taxes, all contributed to escalating disagreements between the secular Turco-Egyptian regime and the intransigent Islamists.

As a result, in 1871 Muhammad Ahmad, a member of the Samaniyya order in Sudan, withdrew to the Aba Island on the White Nile and began recruiting disciples. On June 29, 1881, he proclaimed himself the *Mahdi* (the "guided one" or messianic redeemer of Islam). He declared *jihad* (holy war) against the Khartoum government, promising paradise to those who died in battle. The great slave merchants allied themselves with him, placing their private armies at his disposal. Nomadic tribes, such as the Arab Baggara, also responded to his call.

Withdrawing to the Nuba Mountains, the Mahdi defeated two military contingents sent by the Egyptian government. On September 9, 1882, he attacked El Obeid but was repulsed. Laying siege to the city, he conquered it in January 1883. Among the prisoners were three priests and four nuns, all Comboni missionaries. At the end of 1885, the Mahdi succeeded in capturing Khartoum,[20] which led to the establishment of a Mahdist regime that lasted fourteen years. In 1899, under Lord Kitchener, English counteroffensive put an end to the Mahdist regime in the battle of Omdurman, in the course of which the Mahdi's successor, the caliph Abdullah, was killed. The so-called Anglo-Egyptian joint ownership of Sudan lasted until independence in 1956.

The tattooing

It was customary that slaves bore on their bodies particular marks or grooves in honor of their owner. These marks were obtained through tattoo incisions. Up until now I did not have

[20] The British Governor Charles George Gordon along with the Austrian and Greek consuls and over ten thousand people were slaughtered. The missionaries, however, were spared numerous tortures since the Mahdi designated them heroes because they were willing to die rather than give up their faith.

any tattoos, while my companions had many, also on their faces and arms. Well, one day on a whim the lady of the house decided to give a gift to those who had not been tattooed. There were three of us.

A woman who was an expert in this cruel art was sent for. She led us beneath the portico, with our mistress behind us, whip in hand. The woman prepared a plate of white flour, another with salt, and a razor. She ordered the first among us to stretch out on the ground. Two of the strongest slaves were commanded to hold her, one by the arms and the other by the legs. She bent down over that unfortunate one and with the flour began to make around sixty marks on her stomach. I could see it all happening before my very eyes, thinking that I was next in line.

Once the marks were all made, the woman took the razor, and down it went, cutting each and every mark that had been traced. The poor slave moaned as the blood dripped down from every wound. Once that operation was completed, she took the salt and began rubbing it hard into each wound, so that it would enter inside the cut, making it larger in order for the slits to remain open. What agony, what torment! That unfortunate one trembled all over, and I trembled too, waiting to undergo the same cruel fate.

After the first victim was carried off to bed, it was my turn. I could not move for the life of me, but one look at the lady of the house and at her raised whip immediately made me get on the ground. The woman, having been told to spare my face, began to make six cuts on my breasts and up to sixty on my stomach. Then forty-eight on my right arm. I could not tell you how I felt. It seemed I was dying at every moment, especially when they rubbed in the salt.

Lying in a pool of blood, I was then carried to a bed, where I remained for hours, unconscious. When I regained consciousness, I saw my companions next to me, who in comparison with me *suffered atrociously. For more than a month, the three of us were condemned to stay there, spread out on a mat without a cloth to dry the water that constantly flowed from our wounds, which the salt had left half-open. The scars are still with me. I can honestly say that the reason I did not die was that the Lord miraculously destined me for better things.*

Humiliated yet chaste

There is another episode in Bakhita's youth, during the time spent under the roof of the Turkish general, that gives us a good understanding of how cruel the life of a slave must have been and how much it affected the rest of Mother Josephine's life. The incident, which occurred during adolescence, was so psychologically devastating that the saint had the courage to recount it only in strict confidence in her old age. As a result, it appeared in neither the biography of 1910 nor in Zanolini's *Tale of Wonder*. Nevertheless, it is Zanolini who revealed this information during the beatification process, explaining that it was brought to her attention thanks to a note she had received from Mother Martini, the superior at that time of the Canossian house in Schio, who in turn received the story from another sister in whom Mother Josephine had confided.

We present the testimony released by Ida Zanolini in the course of the ordinary beatification process in Vicenza, certain that the episode transpired more or less as it is described here.

Bakhita came of age and developed harmoniously. The Turkish general was satisfied with her, proud to possess a slave of such racial purity. But one day he said to his wife: "That slave is maturing well, but I don't like the way she sticks out like that."

"In the afternoon," Bakhita recalled, "the master called for me. I ran and knelt down before him, as was the custom. He took the budding part of my chest roughly in his hands and began to twist my breasts as if they were dishrags. I fainted, and for the rest of the day I was left alone. But the next day, and on two other successive days, I underwent the same treatment. The master twisted my already much-tortured flesh, squeezing until every trace of roundness was eliminated. And I had to hold still without complaint, or else I would be whipped. Now I'm like a smooth table.

In recounting this episode, Zanolini emphasized that in the note sent to her by Mother Martini, it was explained that after relating this episode, Bakhita added, "When I was questioned about my life, I did not mention this part, because I was ashamed."

A little earlier, in a casual reference to this episode, Zanolini's testimony at the beatification process mentioned Bakhita's chastity: "In response to my explicit questions on this matter, Mother Bakhita said that none of her masters, and none of the slaves either, had ever touched her." Sister Josephine always gave this same answer over the course of her life, attributing such circumstances to the intercession of Mary and to the protection of her guardian angel.

When one considers the harrowing accounts of cruelty against women that have come to light, it seems impossible that, without direct divine intervention, Bakhita would have been able to preserve her virginity. And she took great pride in this fact. "Mother," she said when already very old, speaking to her superior Martini, "I have been in the middle of mud, but I never got dirty."

From the market to freedom

After being away for several months, the general returned to Kordofan having decided to return definitively to Turkey.[21] He therefore began preparing for the departure. Since he had a large quantity of slaves, he chose ten, and I was among them. He sold the rest. We left Kordofan on camels, and after a number of days traveling we stopped at a hotel in Khartoum. There he sent out word that he had slaves for sale.

The Italian consul [Calisto Legnani] came forward. He asked me to bring him a coffee. He looked me over from head to foot, but I did not think he had any plans of buying me. I learned that he did only the next day, when the Turkish general told me to follow the consul's chambermaid and help her carry a bundle.[22]

This time I was truly lucky, because the new master was very good and was very fond of me. My job was to help the chambermaid with housework. I did not get scolded, punished, or beaten; it did not seem true that one could enjoy such peace and tranquility.

Two years or more passed without any change. Then the consul was suddenly called back to Italy on grave business.[23] I do not know why, but when I heard the name of Italy, of whose beauty and charm I knew nothing, my heart was filled with the most fervent desire—the desire to follow my master. Because he liked me so much, I dared to ask him to bring me to Italy with him. He explained to me how long and expensive the trip would be. But I insisted so much that in the end he consented. I knew later that it

[21] This was the middle of 1882. The general, most likely engaged in a campaign against the Mahdi, returned convinced that the rebels would soon take El Obeid.

[22] As we have seen, it was precisely because of a bundle that Bakhita ended up as the prey of the Arab kidnappers.

[23] At the end of 1884 the Mahdist revolution was spreading across the country. Legnani fled Khartoum, which was conquered by the fundamentalist army a short time later.

was God who wanted this to happen. I can still taste the joy I felt at the time.

And so we left. It was the consul and his friend and a black boy and me. We traveled by camel in a caravan, and after a few days we arrived in Suakin. After about a month, the consul and his friend received bad news that a gang of rebels had entered the city of Khartoum, had devastated everything, and had carried away all the slaves. Both the consul and his friend had been robbed of everything and were utterly dejected. If I had remained there, I certainly would have been stolen, and then what would have happened to me? How grateful to the Lord I was for having saved me yet again.

Farewell to Africa

We stayed in Suakin for a month and then traveled by ship over the Red Sea and other seas until we landed in Genoa. There we found lodging in a hotel owned by a man whom the consul's friend knew very well and who had asked him the favor of acquiring a black boy for him. As a result, the one who had been my travel companion was soon given to this hotel owner.

The wife of the consul's friend, who had come to meet him, saw us blacks and wanted one. She asked her husband why he had not brought one back for her and her daughter. The consul, to please his friend and his wife, gave me to them as a gift.

After a short time we were on the road again. The consul set out for Padua, and I never heard anything about him again. My new owners and I were off to Mirano Veneto, where for three years I was the nanny to their little daughter. This little one liked me a great deal, and I of course reciprocated with equal affection.

At the end of the three years, I returned with my mistress to Suakin in Africa, where her husband maintained a large hotel. I

64

stayed there for about nine months, after which the master decided that the whole family was going to settle there. His wife, however, would return to Italy in order to sell their property and pack up the furniture, while I stayed in the hotel with the little girl. But my mistress did not want to depart by herself and arranged that both her daughter and I should return with her. In my heart, I therefore bid an eternal farewell to Africa. A voice inside me told me that I would never see my continent again.

A story in two versions

Calisto Legnani was born in Menaggio in the northern Italian province of Como. In 1878 he went on business to Sudan, where his primary job was importing Arabian rubber. At the time, El Obeid was the hub of the rubber trade, while Kordofan was the principal rubber producer in the world.[24] Two years later he became the Italian consul in Khartoum, where there were both a large Comboni mission and a Catholic school that were familiar to the Legnanis. It should not be forgotten that Saint Daniel Comboni himself died in Khartoum in 1881.

In his capacity as consul in 1882, Legnani checked into the hotel, where he happened upon the Turkish general—whose acquaintance he had probably already made in El Obeid—and where he proceeded to ransom the young African woman, putting her to work alongside his own housemaid. Ransoming young slaves was a frequent gesture among Europeans who had important tasks in Africa. In all probability, then, Legnani knew Comboni and was influenced by him

---

[24] A book from this time period, *Il paese della gomma* (The rubber country), was written by Demetrio Prada, who was a friend of Legnani's and was the representative in Sudan of a Milanese firm that imported rubber.

in some way. It was not by chance that he brought to Italy not only Bakhita, but also another young former slave from Sudan.

As a businessman and a representative of the Italian government in Sudan, Legnani came to know Augusto Michieli, the friend with whom he fled Khartoum at the end of 1884 and to whom he entrusted Bakhita upon their arrival in Italy in April 1885.

These dates (late 1884/early 1885) are inferred from Bakhita's story, according to which a short time after the group's escape from Khartoum and their arrival in Suakin they received news that the capital of Kordofan had fallen to the rebels. We know that Muhammad Ahmad—the "Mahdi"— entered the city on January 26, 1885, and that in the summer of 1884 he set up his headquarters in the nearby village of Omdurman on the western banks of the Nile, from which point he gradually put the entire capital under siege. Already in March 1884, Gordon Pasha had given the order for Europeans to evacuate the city. Nevertheless, Legnani, Michieli, and their small entourage must have escaped just in the nick of time through a gap in the siege line.

This is the reconstruction of events that has prevailed to this day. However, Father Giuseppe Vantini, a Comboni missionary and a historian of Sudan, maintains that things could have transpired differently. Vantini proposes another scenario, based on the historical work of Massimo Zaccaria, the only person who has done extensive research on Italians in nineteenth-century Sudan. Zaccaria has unearthed four letters signed by Calisto Legnani, which were written and sent from Varignano in the province of Genoa, between August and December 1883.

During this five-month period, therefore, Legnani was in Italy. Having rescued Bakhita from the Turkish general the year before, according to Vantini he could have already brought her to Italy with him and entrusted her to the Michieli family. In support of this claim, the historian Vantini points to a letter by Comboni father Léon Hanriot dated July 14, 1883, which states that Legnani and Michieli departed on July 7—a departure, Vantini maintains, that could have been caused by the collapse of the Italian firm owned by Legnani: the "grave business" to which Bakhita refers.

At any rate, by the end of 1883 Legnani had already traveled back to Sudan and was establishing himself in Suakin as the vice-consul. Michieli was either with him at that time or arrived a few months later. From Suakin, Legnani sent an official letter dated February 16, 1884. During that period it is probable—and almost certain, given his official as well as his commercial responsibilities—that he traveled one or more times to Khartoum together with Michieli, with just enough time to enter and leave without running afoul of the rebels. They then left Suakin for Italy in the early part of 1885, possibly fearing that the Mahdist revolt could spread to the shores of the Red Sea.

Birth certificate data also indicate that Alice Alessandrina Augusta, known as Mimmina, whose nanny was Bakhita, was born in Zianigo di Mirano in the province of Venezia on February 3, 1886. Michieli, therefore, must have returned to Italy in the first half of 1885 (in April, according to Bakhita).

Consequently, Bakhita's story and Vantini's reconstruction are in complete accord, on the condition that Legnani and Michieli brought the two young Sudanese with them to Italy in their second rather than their first trip, after spiriting them safely away, along with their own belongings, from the doomed Khartoum.

The consul's friend and Turina the Russian

Who was this Augusto Michieli who received Bakhita under his care once she arrived in Italy? He was a wealthy businessman and also a professional translator. Hailing from an ancient Venetian family of noble extraction, he was born in Venice on August 2, 1848. His father was from Trent and his mother from Vienna. He married Maria Turina, a Russian from Saint Petersburg. For all intents and purposes she was an atheist, though she was brought up in the Russian Orthodox Church. It was Lady Turina who prevailed upon Legnani in Genoa to give her the young Bakhita.

When spending time in Italy, the Michielis lived at the family villa in Zianigo, in the hamlet of Mirano. It is a house with ample grounds; the address at the time was 136 Via Cavin di Sala. It has since undergone significant renovation and can be found today on Via Bollati. Michieli built a large guesthouse on this property as well, and this is where Bakhita lived for three and a half years, that is, until she entered the Institute of Catechumens in Venice. At first she worked as a maid, and then when Alice was born she became the full-time and much-beloved nanny.

The Michielis had three children. The first, Carlo Alberto Augusto, was born in Paris in 1879. The other two were born in Zianigo. The second, who probably died in infancy and for whom no reliable records exist, had to have been born in the summer of 1884. The last was Alice Alessandrina Augusta (Mimmina), born on February 3, 1886. Several months after her birth, Augusto returned to Suakin and built the guesthouse. Legnani already held the position of vice-consul. The island and port city of Suakin, both under the protection of the British admiral Graham, never fell into the hands of the Mahdist rebels.

Bakhita's return to Suakin, where she worked in the hotel bar and canteen shop, can be dated to the end of 1886. The trip back to Mirano to sell the property took place at the end of the summer of 1887. The Michielis' definitive move to Suakin, and Bakhita's decision to remain in Italy, came in December 1889. Almost twenty years later, after the death of their parents, Mimmina and her brother returned again to Italy. Both married in 1910, Mimmina in Naples and Carlo Alberto in Rome. The relationship with Bakhita came to an end in Venice, as we shall soon see, at the time of the dramatic farewell in 1889.

III

The Great Decision

Checchini the Massarioto: The man between two saints

Before proceeding farther in this journey, it is worthwhile
to pause momentarily upon a figure who will have a profound impact on Bakhita's life and on her religious vocation: Illuminato Checchini, the Michielis' estate manager.

Organizer of Catholic associations and promoter and
founder of credit unions and healthcare insurance programs
for farmers and craftsmen, Illuminato Checchini (also known
under his artistic pseudonym as Stefano Massarioto) was one
of the most well-known men of his time in the Veneto region.
Little more than a peasant, in the 1890s he achieved such
popularity among the people of the countryside that his arrival
in a village was often accompanied by the ringing of bells
and by parties organized in the piazzas with improvised tri-
umphal arches. He is a controversial and much-discussed personality even today. The peasants of his day loved him, while
the liberal and anticlerical bourgeoisie could not abide him.
In those years Checchini blazed an utterly unique trail of
self-transformation, beginning as a barely educated negotiator and consultant for small property owners and peasants
and emerging as an indefatigable storyteller, a moral guide
to peasants, a country orator and writer in dialect with a
rare knack for incisive political commentary, and an author

of books, articles, and almanacs that for long periods were the principal springboards of discussion at the traditional *filò* gatherings. It is a trajectory whose peak was followed almost inevitably by oblivion, where the only comfort was one's family. Checchini's is a small "great provincial story" whose popularity benefited from the fact that he was personally acquainted with a certain village priest and an illiterate black girl, both of whom were elevated to the honor of the altars long after he was forgotten.

Illuminato Checchini was born in Salzano in the province of Venezia in 1840. He was the son of a craftsman who made wagons and carriages. After second grade he began helping his father in the shop. He enjoyed playing the organ in church. He completed his military service in the Austro-Hungarian army. These were the years (1867–1875) when Father Giuseppe Sarto was the parish priest of Salzano, the man who would become patriarch of Venice, then rise to the papal throne with the name of Pius X, and ultimately be canonized in 1954.

Little is known about the relationship between Checchini and Father Giuseppe. What is certain is that these two near contemporaries got along well and that Illuminato's activities in the countryside were inspired, after his own fashion, by Father Sarto's ideas about the social doctrine of the Church. Checchini was the parish organist. Already at this time he displayed a strong activist bent, as did his parish priest. It is said that both men loved to play cards, and on winter nights they could be found enjoying long games together.

The two men began seeing less of one another beginning in 1870, when Checchini married and moved to Zianigo. Here he resided until 1894, in a house that still stands today. In the spring of 1885 he met Bakhita and was probably the first one to nudge her in the direction of the Christian faith.

At this point in time, Checchini was not yet famous. But he was certainly known around Mirano for his activity as a business negotiator, dealmaker in the countryside, estate manager (Augusto Michieli's orchard shared a border with his own property), seller of farm tools, and counselor to peasants and the poor. He became a key reference point for the rural population that was experiencing the transfer of power from the Austro-Hungarian Empire to Piedmont's house of Savoy—a historical transition, with all its accompanying contradictions, whose impact was felt most acutely by the vulnerable social classes and the villages. Whoever could read and write became the natural mediator between the illiterate peasant families[1] and the so-called managerial class.

Checchini's path from an advocate for poor peasants to a tireless voice for peasants' rights was short yet directly linked to his faith-based convictions and his friendship with Giuseppe Sarto (for whom, when Sarto was patriarch of Venice, Checchini performed several administrative tasks in the countryside between the adjoining provinces of Treviso and Venezia). Between 1889 and 1890, in response both to the spread of the liberal and Masonic ideology and the anticlerical activity of the government and ruling elites, the Opera dei congressi—a national lay organization for all types of Catholic social action inspired by the social doctrine promoted by Pope Leo XIII—set in motion the so-called "exit from the sacristy", that is, social initiatives aimed at promoting a Catholic presence in society. In the Veneto region,

[1] Such families were often afflicted with famine and vitamin-deficiency ailments, were oppressed by proprietors and moneylenders, and were threatened and impoverished by volatile economic conditions caused by emigration and military campaigns.

these initiatives occurred largely in the countryside where Checchini took on a leadership role that also coincided with his support of the movement of Catholic intransigents[2] in the Treviso province.

It was precisely in 1889 that Checchini launched into publishing. Under the pseudonym of Paròn Stefano Massarioto,[3] he penned his first almanac, *Massarioto's Almanac for 1890*. Written in dialect, this work contained many satirical pieces on social and political topics. It was an unexpected runaway success.[4] The almanacs, with their popular and enjoyable writing style, concretely addressed everyday problems through simple dialogues and stories and also connected the principles of the Catholic intransigent movement with the spontaneous anti-institutional sentiments of the poor. As a result, Checchini's almanacs became the conversational centerpiece at the nightly peasant gatherings (the so-called *filò*), which took place in the stalls of barns. It was therefore not by chance that Massarioto was fond of saying, with a barely concealed pride, "I write for the stalls."

In 1892 Checchini started writing "for the stalls" with a more direct sociopolitical intent in the pages of the new Catholic weekly *La vita del popolo* (The life of the people).

---

[2] Catholic intransigents declared their solidarity with the Holy Father and the hierarchy, maintaining a critical distance from the state because it had annexed the Papal States and enacted anticlerical laws: Church marriage was not recognized by civil law, religious orders were suppressed and their property confiscated, ecclesiastical welfare associations were secularized, and religious instruction in schools was eliminated. See *The History of the Church*, vol. 9, *The Church in the Industrial Age*, ed. Hubert Jedin (New York: Crossroad, 1981), p. 84.—TRANS.

[3] A rustic-sounding last name typical of sharecroppers, tenant farmers, and small landowners.

[4] With an annual circulation of fifty thousand copies sold in the Veneto region, these almanacs continued to be published even after the author's death.

Edited by Monsignor Luigi Bellio, one of the leaders of the rural Catholic movement, this newspaper was the direct fruit of the revolutionary contents of Pope Leo XIII's *Rerum novarum*, published a year earlier. This encyclical aimed above all to raise mankind out of the contradictions posed by a capitalism without God and "to refute the solution proposed by socialism" so as to resolve the question of workers and peasants through a path indicated by the Church.

It was the task of Massarioto's piquant pen to translate for peasant ears the political and social ideas expounded by Monsignor Bellio on the front page of the newspaper. This editorial combination brought the weekly, like the almanacs, into the hands of the traditional *filò* audience and gained for it a circulation of twenty-five thousand copies.

In those years, therefore, the storytelling flair of Massarioto (antimodernist though he was, as well as intolerant) became a fundamental tool in raising the awareness of the rural masses about their own problems and rights—even as Christians—over against the state.[5] Massarioto's fame peaked between 1895 and 1897. In the countryside he was known by all, and everybody wanted him at their parties and rallies. His almanacs were sold at the markets, at fairs, and at church doors. It was a kind of stardom that worried the liberal ruling class so much that he was subjected to numerous forms of pressure and intimidation. Then, after the state repression of 1898, which extinguished the extremist tendencies of the Catholic intransigents in favor of the clerical-moderate movements, Massarioto's inevitable political decline began, as did the decline of Monsignor Bellio's influence a short time later.

[5] This awareness was an experience that would lead in time to "white" (or Christian-inspired) trade unionism and cooperatives (as opposed to "red" [or socialist] ones).

Checchini's collaboration ceased with *La Vita del Popolo*, which was transformed from a newspaper of the Catholic intransigents into a tranquil diocesan weekly. For a time he joined forces with other diocesan weekly papers. He wrote two novels in dialect that remained in print until 1934. He died on April 11, 1906, in Padua, where he and his family had moved in 1894, as recounted in the long obituary published in the *Messaggero di Sant'Antonio* (*Saint Anthony Messenger*).

From that moment on, oblivion cast its shadow upon this figure, who had become something of an anachronism, and a slightly embarrassing one, even though, as we have seen, the almanacs and novels stayed in print for some time. There has been renewed talk of Massarioto in recent years. As the object of a study by Livio Vanzetto, the historian of the Veneto region—a study published several times also by *La Vita del Popolo*—Checchini has been at the center of a local controversy in the pages of Veneto's daily newspaper, *Il Gazzettino*, on the occasion of the 1992 republication of one of his almanacs. On the basis of the historical record, Massarioto-Checchini's "interventionism" has been stigmatized in particular as anti-Semitic, in reference to a bitter debate in 1896 in the pages of *La Vita del Popolo* against the then candidate for mayor of Mirano, Paolo Errera, who was Jewish and who eventually won the election.[6] This demonstrated that the newspaper's stance, as well as that of Massarioto, was not merely the result of clerical Catholic conditioning but was motivated rather by a critical spirit in the service of political and social transformation. It should also not be forgotten that on many occasions Massarioto railed against the scourge of usury (in this context, rural

[6] Only those who could afford to pay an annual tax had the right to vote. Universal voting rights for men were introduced only in 1912.

credit unions and their "look-alikes", which were largely controlled by Jews). At the same time, however, it also needs to be recalled that the way in which Checchini and his family welcomed the black Bakhita like a daughter, in the face of the prejudices and curiosity that were second nature in that epoch, is surely nothing short of prophetic and the farthest thing from racism.

Checchini and Bakhita

It is to this one-of-a-kind peasant-polemicist that Bakhita owed her first knowledge of Christ as well as a certain facility for the quick verbal comeback, which she exhibited on more than one occasion, albeit in complete humility, even when responding to questions from superiors.

Checchini was certainly the first person to take a personal interest in her Christian formation. He was the one who gave Bakhita her first crucifix. He is the one who invited Michieli's maid, against the wishes of her mistress, to recite her daily prayers with the young African. He is also the one who accompanied Bakhita along the successive stages in her journey of faith, always ready to help her pay her catechumen's fee and to give her hospitality in his house whenever the need arose. He is the one who supported her decision to enter religious life, even though his fatherly love for the girl went so far as to offer her a dowry, as one would for a daughter, in case she decided to remain in his house. "A man with a heart of gold and an upright conscience", affirmed Bakhita in 1910. It is not surprising, therefore, that Bakhita remained extremely fond of Checchini all her life, calling him "Daddy" and considering his children her brothers and sisters.

Bakhita maintained fairly frequent contact with Checchini's children and grandchildren through correspondence on postcards and holy cards that she dictated to one of her religious sisters.[7]

In one of these letters, belonging to Maria Pia Checchini, a descendant of both Illuminato and Saint Pius X's sister (Illuminato's firstborn son, Giuseppe, married Enrica De Bei, daughter of Antoniasa Sarto, the Pope's sister), written at Schio on February 7, 1927, and addressed to "Dearest Ines", Mother Josephine dictated the following lines: "How happy I would be to see you, dearest Ines, and to see all of those whom I hold as my own family. I will make up for it with my prayers . . . Take heart, then: let us work, suffer, pray, and become saints, for this is the one thing necessary."

Maria Pia Checchini has also saved a keepsake that Bakhita addressed to her on the day of Maria Pia's first Communion. It consists of a little image about the size of a holy card, which depicts Jesus at the altar, surrounded by angels, giving first Communion to a little girl on her knees, with her guardian angel by her side. On the back, a handwritten note at the bottom reads: "Remember with love the first kiss from Jesus", signed "Sister Josephine Bakhita".

Maria Pia has also preserved for posterity two beautiful handmade objects that the young Bakhita probably made during her stay in Venice and then gave to Illuminato's fam-

---

[7] Bakhita knew only how to read. Almost nothing remains of this epistolary activity except a postcard preserved in the little Bakhita museum in the Canossian house in Schio, along with some notes and letters that are privately owned.

ily as gifts (during her long residency at Schio, Mother Jose-phine also loved to make things by hand from time to time). The two objects are a little change purse and a doily made entirely of multicolored glass beads threaded and woven together in various designs.

The little crucifix

The incident that stands out more than any other in Bakh-ita's relationship with Checchini has to do with the little crucifix.

It took place at the end of the summer of 1888. After trying for nearly a year, Lady Maria Turina succeeded in selling the house in Zianigo with its surrounding property. The registered bill of sale carries the date of July 19.[8] Hav-ing sold the house, she decided to return to Africa, where her husband awaited her in Suakin at the hotel he had acquired two years earlier and that he now ran. This was only a temporary move, for they knew she had to return to Italy one more time in order to make other final arrange-ments. It was unnecessary as well as risky to make their daughter, who was not yet three years old, go on two more long trips in such a short time. It was decided, therefore, that the daughter would stay in Italy with Bakhita, in whom they placed their full trust, knowing how much she loved their little girl. They consulted friends and asked Checchi-ni's advice as well. The latter strongly recommended that Mimmina and Bakhita take up residence at the boarding school run by the Canossian Sisters at the Institute of Catechumens in Venice, for he sensed that this might be a

[8] Deed no. 2707, registered by the notary public Pantoli di Noale.

way to introduce Bakhita to Christianity in a way that would safely circumvent Turina's religious prohibitions.

Lady Turina vacillated, recounted Bakhita,

for more than a month, without arriving at a decision. The lady's estate manager, Mr. Illuminato Checchini, then intervened . . .

It was during the course of this month, perhaps facilitated by Checchini's more frequent visits to the Michieli house, that he presented Bakhita with a little silver crucifix. According to Mother Josephine, this was an event of profound importance for her:

As he gave me the crucifix he kissed it with devotion, then explained that Jesus Christ, the Son of God, had died for me. I did not know what a crucifix was, but I was moved by a mysterious power to keep it hidden, out of fear that the lady would take it away. I had never hidden anything before, because I had never been attached to anything. I remember that I looked at it in secret and felt something inside that I could not explain.

This seemingly innocuous event is all the more extraordinary because of how much it dovetailed with the spirituality of Saint Magdalene of Canossa and the Canossian Rule. The reference to Christ Crucified is a constant in Saint Magdalene's thought: "Seek God alone and Christ Crucified" is the internal fulcrum around which the Rule rotates. In Saint Magdalene's *Memoirs*, a kind of diary she kept as a young girl in which she recorded her observations about her journey of faith, the founder of the Canossians writes: "In creating the rules of the Daughters of Charity, I intend to take the virtues of the Cross." Later, writing to a sister during one her many trips to the already-numerous houses spread around the world, she affirms: "I desire for you and your dear companions every happiness, namely, that you seek and find God alone, so that the Crucified alone is the one happiness of the Daughters of Charity."

It was precisely in the large crucifix hanging in the parlor of the Institute of Catechumens that Bakhita found the strength to oppose Lady Turina. Upon the latter's return to Italy, after nearly a year's absence, Mrs. Turina Michieli demanded that her servant give up her plans for baptism and return definitively to Africa with her and Mimmina.

Memories as a catechumen

Bakhita later recalled, in reference to the days immediately preceding her admittance to the house of catechumens, when it was a matter of trying to persuade Mrs. Michieli to let them lodge there,

Mr. Illuminato was so concerned that I should be admitted to the Institute of Catechumens that he gave his written word on a stamped document that, in the unlikely event that the lady did not fulfill her obligation, [with regard to paying for her daughter Mimmina's room and board] *he would pay for it himself.*

And thus, with his wife and five children and Mrs. Michieli, Illuminato Checchini accompanied the young Bakhita and the little girl to Venice.

In this way we were both received at the house of catechumens. The little girl and I were entrusted to the care of a nun, Maria Fabbretti, who was in charge of catechetical instruction.

I am unable to remember without tears how well she took care of me. She wanted to know if I desired to become a Christian, and sensing that I did and that I had come there with that intention, she was overjoyed. So those holy mothers instructed me with heroic patience and introduced me to that God who from childhood I had felt in my heart without knowing who he was. I remembered [in her village in Africa] *looking at the moon and stars and the beautiful things in nature and saying to myself, "Who is the master of all these beautiful things?" And I experienced a great desire to see him and know him and honor him. And now I do know him. Thank you, thank you, my God!*

At this point in the story, Mother Josephine turned momentarily to the time when Lady Turina took her and Mimmina to Venice.

When the lady brought me to the boarding school, on the doorstep as she turned to say goodbye, she said, "Here you are; this is your home." She said it just like that, without understanding the deeper meaning of these words. Oh, if she could have imagined how much would happen to me, she would never have brought me there.

The impact of Venice

No one who has told Bakhita's story has ever placed much importance on the impact of the Italian reality upon the young African woman from her arrival at the port of Genoa onward. Traveling from the arid climate of sub-Saharan Africa, she boarded the *Rubattino*, a shipping company vessel that made navigational history, and sailed through the Suez Canal to the largest port in the Mediterranean. Bakhita was a black immigrant in Italy during a time when thousands of poor families were fleeing precisely from Genoa in search of better fortunes overseas. A daughter of the dry savannahs, Bakhita traversed the Apennines of Liguria in the bloom of springtime, probably by train, and crossed the Po River valley in order to reach the Veneto region.

No one has given much importance to the impressions that the long stay in the extraordinary city of Venice must have made on Bakhita, a city not so far geographically from Africa yet worlds away from the culture she had known and experienced before.

Leaving to our imagination what it must have been like to experience the "city on water" for the first time, let us concentrate instead for a moment on the little room that Bakhita and Mimmina shared at the Institute of Catechumens. This room still exists today and is used as the bedroom for one of the Salesian Sisters who now run the house. The room is very bright yet barely big enough for two beds. The view from the window is almost completely filled by the cupola of the Basilica of Santa Maria della Salute (Our Lady of Salvation).[9] This particular fact helps explain why Mother Bakhita warmly recalled many years later that her room was nestled "under the shadow of the Madonna".

As she became acquainted with her new environment, Bakhita surely would have asked her catechist and tutor, the beloved Sister Fabbretti, about the stone structure she could see from her window every day. Considering how important the Madonna della Salute has always been to Venice, Sister Fabbretti certainly would have offered a

---

[9] The Italian term *salute* denotes not only "salvation" but also "safety" and "health". Thus, the basilica's name can also be read as Our Lady of Safety or Our Lady of Health.—TRANS.

generous explanation. She would have recounted that the inhabitants of the city had decided to build and dedicate this large church to the Mother of Jesus in thanksgiving for having halted the great plague of 1630. It is a story of love, fear, and devotion surely capable of stimulating Bakhita's already-strong desire to learn more about the mysteries of Christianity. The story would have introduced her to the popular religiosity of the Venice of that time, which drew upon numerous episodes of divine intervention and abounded with saints to whom people turned in time of difficulty or need.

The image of the Madonna and Child venerated in the basilica is a Byzantine icon that was brought to Venice in 1670 from the shrine of Saint Titus in Crete. It is an image before which Bakhita probably stopped and prayed when she took Mimmina out on walks during free time. A black Madonna, as is frequently the case in Byzantine iconography, the Madonna della Salute bears in her arms a little black Jesus. Just like Bakhita.

The Institute of Catechumens

The boarding house for catechumens, including Bakhita's room, along with the Church of Saint John the Baptist and the baptismal font at which the young African woman was baptized can be found today, as they were then, at numbers 107/108 Rio terrà dei catechumeni. Instead of the Canossian Sisters, the Sisters of Saint Francis de Sales now run the house. The edifice no longer offers hospitality to adults of diverse nationalities and religions who were prepared for baptism in the heyday of the Most Serene Republic, as Venice was once called. Instead, today there is a kindergarten as well as a residence hall for college students that accommodates up to forty women in the same rooms that were once occupied by catechumens.

The Institute of Catechumens was born on October 21, 1557. When the chief magistrate, or doge, of Venice was Lorenzo Priuli and the patriarch was Vicenzo Diedo, a group of seven citizens was inspired to launch an institution, similar to the one founded a year earlier by Saint Ignatius of Loyola in Rome, that would prepare non-Christian adults who desired to learn about the Catholic religion and be baptized.[10] The first catechumens were given accommodations in a house near the parish of Saints Ermagora and Fortunato. The administration of the house was overseen by a board of clerics, nobles, and citizens. However, following the victorious naval battle of Lepanto in 1571, the non-Christians who came to Venice become so numerous that more space needed to be found. With the help of thirty benefactors, a larger structure was purchased, and the institute was housed in this building. It was a house comprised of two separate wings, one for women and one for men. It was constructed around the present Church of Saint John the Baptist.

Very soon this new edifice also became too small. In 1636, when eighty catechumens were baptized, such attention was paid to the institute by the Most Serene Republic that the nobles were competing to become godparents to the newly baptized.[11]

[10] The institute's first constitution specified further that neophytes, once they received baptism, would never leave the house "unless they were provided with similar lodging arrangements".

[11] The doge at the time, a man by the name of Gritti, went so far as to confer upon his godson, a baptized Jew, both knighthood and the family coat of arms.

The building was reconstructed and expanded in 1727 following the architectural plan of Giorgio Massari. Especially noteworthy were the columned courtyard and the spiral staircase leading to the upper floors (the same staircase Bakhita would have climbed to reach her room), which was not designed with a central pillar but was rather a self-supporting structure made of overlapping stone steps. The vault of the ceiling above the stairwell was decorated with a fresco of the baptism of Jesus, as was the altarpiece in the church, painted by Leandro Bassano.

As Venice's power began to wane, so did the number of catechumens. In 1848 the institute adjusted to this loss of vitality by entrusting the administration of the girls' wing to the Canossian Sisters, who opened a free school for poor girls in the neighborhood (the Sisters of Saint Francis de Sales acquired this school in 1930). Similarly a prior oversaw the boys' wing. Upon the arrival of the Canossians, several Venetian noblewomen began to meet together with them for prayers and spiritual exercises. It was in this context that Bakhita and Mimmina were admitted to the house at the very end of 1888 or the beginning of 1889.

A few months earlier, in 1888, the little church on the institute's grounds had become a pilgrimage destination due to the presence of a statue, still on display to this day, of Our Lady of La Salette that had recently been crowned by the cardinal patriarch of Venice, Domenico Agostini, at the behest of Pope Leo XIII. On the ground floor, in the parlor (now transformed into a chapel), one can still find hanging from the same wall a large crucifix before which Bakhita, as we shall see, prayed for strength in order to resist the demands of Lady Turina, who wanted to take her back to Africa.

The test

Bakhita and Mimmina settled into their new surroundings
with joy, lovingly cared for by the sisters. Thanks to Mother
Maria Fabbretti, the young African girl was introduced to
the principles of the Christian faith in a clear and systematic way. This was no easy task, given the fact that Bakhita
could neither read nor write. In addition, she expressed herself only in the most rudimentary manner, using a curious
patchwork language: half Venetian dialect and half Italian.
What she was able to learn, however, gave her the firm
conviction that she wanted to be baptized. In particular,
Bakhita was struck by the explanations that gradually unfolded
and illuminated the meaning of the words Checchini had
spoken when he gave her the crucifix: about how Jesus
Christ, the Son of God, died for us. Sister Marietta explained
that Jesus loves all of us, all of us equally, and he wants each
one of us to become a child of God. These words were not
easy to grasp for one who had lived nearly her whole life as
a slave and had grown up under masters as if she were an
inferior being, an animal without rights, to be punished at
will and never loved. These were words that left an indel-
ible imprint upon her heart, much deeper than the many
tattoos cut into her scarred flesh.

It was during this period of serenity and interior growth
that the arrival of Mrs. Turina Michieli took place. Nine
months had passed, maybe a year. Lady Turina came back
from Suakin in order to settle the lingering administrative
matters in her family affairs and then to return permanently to Africa with her daughter and black servant. Back
at the hotel in Suakin, in fact, a job was ready and waiting
for the young African girl—behind a bar counter, serving
coffee and liquor. With this objective Mrs. Michieli set out

for the Institute of Catechumens in Venice. However, it was here that she encountered the unexpectedly indomitable will of Bakhita, which asserted itself once again.[12] Bakhita decided that she would not return to Africa, convinced that she would not be allowed to be baptized there and would be unable to use the "treasure", in the Gospel sense, that she had discovered and for which she was ready to give up everything in the world. An argument ensued that eventually went so far as to include such figures as the cardinal, a top military officer, and the king's lawyer, not to mention the large crucifix in the parlor.

But let us listen to Bakhita's account of this episode, keeping well in mind that the references to time indicate only the general sequence of events rather than the actual chronological time that elapsed between them.

Nearly nine months later Lady Turina came to lay claim to her rights on me.

I refused to go back to Africa with her because I was not yet well instructed for baptism. I also thought that, even if I had been baptized already, it would not have been equally possible to profess my new religion and that therefore it was better for me to stay with the sisters.

The lady flew into a rage, accusing me of being ungrateful in making her go back alone, after she had done so much for me.

But I remained firm in my thinking.

She gave me one reason after another, but I would not bend to any of them. And yet it hurt to see her so disgusted with me, for I truly loved her.

[12] For the second time in her life. We recall that the first occasion took place in Khartoum, when she insisted on being taken to Italy by the Italian consul.

It was the Lord who filled me with such firmness, because he wanted to make me all his. O goodness!

The next day she returned in the company of another lady, and she tried to change my mind again with the harshest threats. But to no avail.

They went away greatly vexed.

The reverend superior of the institute, Father Jacopo de' Conti Avogadro di Soranzo, wrote to His Eminence the patriarch Domenico Agostini about this situation. The latter turned to the king's attorney general, who replied by saying that, since I was in Italy, where the slave trade is not allowed, I was in fact quite free.

Lady Turina also went to the attorney general of the king, thinking that she could prevail upon him to agree with her, but she received the same response.

On the third day, she returned to the institute again, accompanied by the same lady and by her brother-in-law, a military officer. Others were present as well, even His Eminence the patriarch Domenico Agostini, the president of the Congregation of Charity, the superior of the institute, and some of the sisters of the catechumenate.

The patriarch spoke first. A long discussion followed, which ended in my favor.

Weeping with rage and sorrow, Lady Turina took her little girl, who could not bear to be separated from me and who tried to make me go with her. I was so upset that I was unable to speak a word. I left crying and withdrew, happy that I had not given in.

It was November 29, 1889.

Up to this point we have the unadorned account of Bakhita, by nature reserved and a person of few words, always ready to downplay the events in her life. For example, she does not mention having asked for help again and again in front of the parlor crucifix during those days. This is a detail she subsequently revealed to several sisters and to Ida Zanolini, who made reference to it in *Tale of Wonder*. For the young African woman, it was a question of engaging in a battle well beyond her simple capacities, a battle that was waged against her over the course of days and that made use of all the authorities and weapons available, including emotions, psychological pressure, guilt, moral claims, and social and cultural heritage.

From all of the testimonies we have, it is clear that Bakhita found that she had to say no to Lady Turina, to Mimmina (who cried desperately at the thought of losing her nanny), and even to the sisters, who at a certain point tried to convince her to follow Mrs. Michieli, sure that the lady thought well of Bakhita. It was a situation fraught with such psychological pressure (in the form of requests coming from persons who loved her and whom she loved in turn) that the only way Bakhita was able to muster the strength to persevere was by asking the Lord for help. And his help, according to direct testimonies, transformed the timid and submissive African into a woman of determination: "No, I will not leave the house of the Lord. It would mean my ruin." This concept of "ruin" would be repeated by Bakhita every time she recounted this episode on other occasions.

During that short year at the institute, Bakhita's idea of dedicating her life to God had already matured to some extent, even though she was not sure whether she could do so in the same way as the sisters who guided her toward baptism, since she would be the only black person among so many whites. Furthermore, after being kidnapped, Bakhita had had a terrible experience of Africa, and it was only by accident or through the Lord's help that she did not lose her life or her purity. Her subsequent brief return to Suakin with the Michieli family had given Bakhita the opportunity to weigh what it would mean to work behind the bar of a hotel in an African port on the Red Sea at a time when the recent opening of the Suez Canal had turned that geographical area into the perfect meeting place for half of the world's adventurers. It was a city in which religious practice was certainly not the principal objective of its European residents and where the hotels often resembled brothels.

From all of these considerations, the desire was born in Bakhita to remain in Italy. It was a desire that, joined with her constant plea for help from Christ Crucified, became transformed into a firm and irrevocable resolve. Thus, in a society where social hierarchies still constituted insurmountable barriers, it just so happened that a young, illiterate black woman succeeded in standing up for her rights and in mobilizing the highest religious, civil, and military authorities. In addition to Cardinal Agostini, the king's attorney general, and the high-ranking officer in the Michieli family, the parlor of the Institute of Catechumens where Bakhita's fate was decided also boasted the presence of the prefect, the powerful noblewoman and friend of Lady Turina Michieli, the superior of the institute, the superior of the Canossians, and the president of the Congregation of Charity.

Baptism

A month after these events, Bakhita received the sacraments of baptism, confirmation, and first Holy Communion. It was January 9, 1890. In the little church belonging to the Institute of Catechumens, the highest nobility of Venice gathered together. Illuminato Checchini, who was not yet well known but already signed his name as Stefano Massarioto, was present with his family.

Bakhita described this pivotal day with sparse, unassuming words.

I entered the catechumenate and, having completed the course of instruction, I received—with a joy only the angels could describe—holy baptism.

I took the names Giuseppina, Margherita, and Fortunata,[13] which in Arabic means Bakhita. On the same day I received confirmation and Communion. Oh, what an unforgettable day!

Josephine Margherita Fortunata received baptism, confirmation, and Communion from Cardinal Agostini. Following the tradition of the Institute of Catechumens, the godfather and godmother were Venetian nobles. Accompanying her at the altar was the mother superior, who represented her parents. The godfather was Count Marco Avogadro di Soranzo, at the express request of his wife, Josephine, who was unable to leave her house due to illness. It is not by accident that the first name received at her baptism was Josephine. The second, Margaret, was the name of Mrs. Donati, her sponsor for confirmation.

Regarding the period of Bakhita's catechumenate, it is well worth reporting one of the rare testimonies of her catechist, Sister Fabretti:[14] "Her preparation for baptism was lived completely in the presence of God. She was happy above all else to be considered worthy of becoming a child of God. When I asked her whether she truly wanted to

[13] Josephine, Margaret, and Fortunata (*fortunata* is the Italian term for "lucky").—TRANS.
[14] Sister Marietta Fabretti, who died in 1910, was fifty-seven years old when Bakhita and Mimmina arrived at the institute.

know the Lord, she responded, 'Yes!' I was struck by the tremendous joy that was inside of that Yes."

On the road of holiness

According to the age-old practice of the Institute of Catechumens, the neophyte, once baptized, was to remain there another year in order to gain a complete understanding of the Catholic faith. Bakhita thus remained, even though Checchini, on the same day of her baptism, in the course of the celebrations that followed, took her aside to remind her that he was ready to welcome her into his home as one of his children.

That year also passed, and the young African woman had to ask Mother Fabretti and the superior for the opportunity to stay another year. The congregation willingly agreed, and Bakhita was welcomed warmly, also because the sisters realized that the decision not to return to her former life was a sign that Bakhita might have a religious vocation. Other signs were not long in emerging in the context of direct inquiries.

After months of doubts, prayers, and sufferings, Josephine was unable to keep her vocational aspiration to herself any longer. She confided in Mother Fabretti as well as in her confessor. Thirty years later she spoke about the nature of her anguish with Ida Zanolini:

I did not know how to explain myself. I felt unworthy. I was convinced that since I was of the black race, I would disfigure the congregation and I would not be accepted.

From the day of her baptism to the day of her entry into the novitiate, Bakhita spent four years in the house of catechumens. It was a place where, for the first time since she was made a slave, she felt completely at peace and found emotional and spiritual comfort. And this was due not only to the human warmth and profound openness of Mother Fabretti. It was the gradual discovery of her own spiritual and mystical dispositions that steadily filled her with joy. It was at the Institute of Catechumens that the young African woman began in a prayerful dialogue to become familiar with the *Paròn* and with our Lady, both of whom, step by step, came to take the place of father and mother in her "orphan's" life. It was here that the long periods of meditation began: before Christ Crucified, before the tabernacle, before the Madonna's image.

Several decades later, returning to the institute, Bakhita confided in a friend as they stood in front of the little baptismal font in the Church of Saint John the Baptist: "It was right here that I became a child of God—me, a poor black girl, me, a poor black girl." And on the second floor, in the little shrine dedicated to Our Lady of La Salette, she recalled that, as an orphan, for her "to have our Lady as a mom is a great comfort."

The four years at the institute were interrupted only by a brief period between the summer and fall of 1893, spent at Checchini's home in Zianigo. These were the three months that directly preceded her entrance into the novitiate.

The entire course of these events—from her first inklings of a religious vocation to her profession of vows—was recounted by Bakhita herself.

I remained at the catechumenate four years, during which time a gentle voice in the depths of my soul became clearer and clearer, quickening my desire to become a religious. At last I told my confessor about it. He suggested that I speak with the superior of the house, Sister Luigia Bottesella, who then wrote to the superior of the motherhouse in Verona, Mother Anna Previtali.

The good mother not only granted the request but added that she herself would like to clothe me with the holy habit and, when the time came, receive my profession of vows.

On December 7, 1893, I entered the novitiate, in that very house of the catechumens in Venice. After a year and a half, I was called to Verona for the holy clothing. A few months before completing three years, I returned to Verona, where I professed holy vows on December 8, 1896. In this way God fulfilled the desire of Mother Previtali, who, a month later, on January 11, 1897, went to the next life.

Having received the medal of Our Sorrowful Mother[15] from Reverend Mother Superior, who was very pleased, I entered the community. It was the day of the feast of the Immaculate Conception, 1896. Since that day I have spent fourteen years in religious life, during which I have come to know God's goodness toward me more and more. [These were the final words Bakhita dictated at the end of her 1910 autobiography.]

That day in 1896, like the day of her baptism, was marked by much celebration. The family of Illuminato Checchini, who had now become very well known, was in attendance. The eighty-seven-year-old Luigi Cardinal di Canossa, bishop of the city, desired at all costs to receive Bakhita in his palace, the same edifice that left its mark on the turbulent childhood of the foundress of the Daughters of Charity.[16] It was almost a passing of the baton on the road to holiness.

[15] The image that the Canossians still wear to this day around their necks. At this time it was made of glass and was much venerated.
[16] The nephew of Magdalene, Luigi di Canossa, was the son of Bonifacio di Canossa, the saint's brother.

At left: Illuminato Checchini

Below: Giuseppe Sarto (Pope Pius X)

Mother Josephine Bakhita on the day of her first profession of religious vows in Verona on December 8, 1896. Below is the autograph signature that appears on the back of the photo.

In più sopra il porticato vi era la camera di Bakhita, una bella cameretta ariosa e profumata dai fiori che si arrampicavano fin sotto la finestra.

Three images of the Michieli house in Zianigo di Mirano.

Above: The complete façade as it appeared in the early 1900s.

At left: Detail of the window of Bakhita's room.

Below: The house as it looks today.

The Institute of Catechumens in Venice on Rio Terrà dei Catecumeni

The baptismal font where Bakhita was baptized on January 9, 1890.

Carissima Ines

Schio 9-2-929

Il Signore ha voluto proprio visitare la tua famiglia, con una nuova sciagura, e immagino l'angoscia del vostro cuore. So però che lo spirito di fede è ben radicato in tutti e ciò è un grande conforto perché ci fa vedere i nostri cari lassù, nel bel paradiso, ove non si conosce dolore e da dove ci guardano, ci proteggono, e pregano per noi. Verrà un giorno

che potremo rivederli, riabbracciarli e godere della loro compagnia per sempre.

Ho saputo che Irene ha una bambina e sono contenta stia bene, le ho anche scritto, ma presto le scriverò ancora.

La morte della M. Antonietta fu un dolore anche per noi, perché la conoscevamo tanto buona. Fu una morte veramente santa ed ora gode il premio delle sue virtù.

Ecco la sorte che aspetta a pochi anni di patimento sofferto per amor di Dio, poi un gaudio eterno. Coraggio adunque; lavoriamo, soffriamo, preghiamo e facciamoci sante, che questa è la sola unica cosa necessaria.

Come sarei contenta di vederla, carissima Ines, e di veder tutti i loro che tengo come famiglia mia. Supplirò colla preghiera e lei pure ricordi. L'affma

M. Giuseppina Bachita
F.D.C.C

Above: Bakhita's letter (dictated to a sister) to Ines, Checchini's niece, on the occasion of Mother Antonietta's death.

On the page at left: The crucifix given to Bakhita by Illuminato Checchini.

Above: Saint Magdalene of Canossa (foundress of the Daughters of Charity) in a painting from the middle of the nineteenth century.

At left: Bakhita in one of the three photographs taken by Bruner in Venice in 1933.

Above: The façade of the Canossian house on Via Fusinato in Schio

Left: The interior of the chapel that houses Bakhita's remains.

Below: Bakhita's room.

Above: Bakhita and the community of Schio in 1926.

Below: Bakhita and a class of schoolchildren from Milan during one of her journeys to promote the foreign missions in 1937.

On the page at right: Bakhita with a group of students in Milan and in Vimercate.

Ricorda con amore il pri-
mo bacio di Gesù —.

Suor Giuseppina Bachita
† d.c.c.

A holy card with the words "Remember with love the first kiss of Jesus" sent by Bakhita to Maria Pia Checchini on the day of her first Communion.

Above: Bakhita at Vimercate in 1938.

Below: The printed card in remembrance of Bakhita's fiftieth anniversary of religious life.

Schio, 8 dicembre 1943.

La R. M. GIUSEPPINA BACHITA

fiore del deserto africano - da mani brutali rapito nel suo sbocciare, venduto e martoriato, ma dall'Infinito Amore raccolto e trapiantato in Italia - celebra oggi

IL 50° DI SUA VITA RELIGIOSA
tra le Figlie della B. Maddalena di Canossa

che fin dal 1890 - nella Casa dei Catecumeni a Venezia e in questa di Schio - l'avvolse in un nimbo di grazie rendendola a tutti carissima.

Ai molti che la conoscono il presente ricordo, alla prediletta Festeggiata i voti e gli auguri dell'intero Istituto.

Omaggio dell'Istituto Canossiano, Via Fusinato, che ha l'onore di averla da 43 anni.

FOTO GRAMOLA - SCHIO

Above: The school of the Canossian mission in El Obeid, Sudan.

Below: South Sudanese refugees in the Jabarona camp north of Khartoum.

At left: Mother Scilla Mari in Verona on the occasion of the opening of the process to investigate the miracle, June 6, 1990. In the background, Bishop Giuseppe Amari.

Below: Eva Da Costa Onishi with the prayer group that attested to the miracle.

At bottom: The Church of Mozamboi in Sierra Leone consecrated to Bakhita in 1994.

The crowd of faithful in Saint Peter's Square on the occasion of the beatification of Bakhita and of Escrivà de Balaguer on May 17, 1992.

The patriarch's exam

At this juncture it is worth taking a quick glance back to the days in Venice that preceded Bakhita's journey to Verona, where she made her religious vows. It was the practice in those years for those who aspired to take religious vows to present themselves before a representative of the Church in order to be examined on their reasons for entering religious life. The one to examine Bakhita—possibly because he had heard about this African girl who several years earlier had marshaled all of the Venetian authorities, including his predecessor, and possibly because he had spoken about her with his friend Checchini and wanted to have firsthand knowledge about her spiritual qualities—was none other than the cardinal patriarch of Venice himself, Giuseppe Sarto.

Giuseppe Sarto was born in Riese in 1835 to a family of extremely humble origins. Before becoming bishop of Mantua in 1884, he served as a priest in various capacities in the Veneto region. Up until his episcopal ordination, his work was marked by a passion to promote new religious fervor in the faithful in order to counter the growing liberal and socialist ideologies. It was no accident that his nomination as patriarch of Venice, firmly desired by Pope Leo XIII, was strongly contested by the Italian government. In those years the Veneto region was undergoing a period of great moral and civic turmoil, and the active presence of Sarto, as well as his links with Catholic Action, certainly made him an unwelcome figure in the eyes of the state. Elected pope in 1903, he took the name Pius X.

The impact of Pius X upon the Church was characterized by simplicity, humility, religious piety, the desire to give life to a new season of faith, and, at the same time, by firmness and intransigence. With firmness, in the face of the modernist crisis, he defended the social validity of Christian principles. In this regard, he was famous for his encyclical *Pascendi*. He expressly asked Christians to take up the task of finding "ever better ways of developing the kingdom of God in individuals, families, and society". He denounced every form of nationalism and socialism and forcefully condemned every form of anti-Semitism. To bishops he wrote, "Bend down and be attentive toward the suffering; let no lament find you indifferent. But also preach with ardor to the great and to the small alike about their responsibilities. It is your task to form the consciences of the people and of the public authorities." He reminded them that "in these times of social and intellectual anarchy ... the City cannot be built otherwise than as God has built it." Therefore, he exhorted, citing Saint Paul: "Omnia instaurare in Christo (Restore all things in Christ)."

He died in August 1914, two weeks after having written a heartfelt appeal to world leaders (*Dum Europa fere omnis*) that they strive to avoid the outbreak of what would be the First World War. Pius X was canonized in 1952.

It is this great and humble figure of the Veneto region and of holiness, who was to a certain degree close to Illuminato Checchini, who thus found himself examining Bakhita on the reasons for her choice of religious life.

We have no direct testimonies about this encounter between saints that took place at the Institute of Catechumens—the prince of the Church and the African ex-slave, united by their humble origins and their strong faith, in dialogue in the parlor or in the church before the statue of our Lady. We have no way of knowing what each one thought of the other, what they spoke about together, or what prayers they recited together. History gives us only the brief words of esteem spoken by the patriarch as he bid Josephine farewell: "Make your holy vows without fear. Jesus wants you to; Jesus loves you. Love and serve him always."

IV

A Sister to the People

With the end of what Bakhita herself recounted about her life, the part of her story consisting of adventure and extraordinary events also ends. From 1896, the year of her religious vows, to 1947, the year of her death, Mother Jospehine lived the life of a humble sister, almost exclusively within her convent. This long fifty-one-year period was invariably spent between Venice and Schio, except for three or four years, when she was sent throughout central Italy to promote the missions.

There is a great deal of biographical material that covers this period. Many testimonies exist, enough to fill much more than a single book. What these testimonies almost always lack, however, are specific dates or, alternately, the typical kinds of references to historical events that help situate a famous person within the context of his era. Most of the episodes recounted by people who knew Bakhita contain no references to time and thus do not constitute biographical reference points in the chronological sense of the term. Rather, such episodes deal with the strictly personal relationship between Bakhita and God or between Bakhita and the people around her. They are the fruit of the admiration and wonder that this woman aroused in the persons she met. Testimonies of this sort, transmitted orally or in writing without any biographical pretense, have succeeded in communicating and fostering the perception of sanctity that many people felt and continue to feel in Bakhita's presence.

It is best, however, to avoid setting these kinds of accounts within a historical context that would restrict their human and spiritual meaning. We will present them instead within a thematic framework that accords them ample space to convey the sense of holiness that flowed from Bakhita—the way this holiness was experienced both by those who knew her in the past and by those today who are inspired by her life and example and who invoke her intercession.

For strictly biographical purposes, we will now present a rapid sketch of episodes and of historical events linked to them. This will allow us to lay out a temporal sequence for the specific purpose of developing these episodes and events in the following chapter, as they merit. It should not be forgotten that, if the first part of Bakhita's life is what typically arouses people's curiosity and their desire to know more about her, it is the fifty subsequent years that transform the initial sympathy into an appreciation of her reputation for holiness, a reputation Bakhita received well before her death.

Cook, sacristan, portress

From 1896 to 1902 Bakhita remained in Venice at the Institute of Catechumens, where she lived the life of a novice, largely in seclusion, with a good portion of her day devoted to needlework, weaving at the loom, and working with Murano glass beads—little things to be sold to support the missions or made as religious ornaments.

These are also the years in which her newfound faith and serenity sank deep roots[1] through prayer and the affectionate instructions of Mother Fabbretti.

It should not be forgotten that at the Institute of Catechumens the Canossians were also in charge of hospitality and social service for orphans and girls. As much as her capabilities allowed, Bakhita was certainly involved in this work as well. At the house of catechumens, then, Bakhita was surrounded by signs of her own redemption. There was the huge parlor crucifix; the Basilica of Our Lady of Salvation with the black Madonna; the baptismal font, place of definitive access to God's love; and the statue of Our Lady of La Salette, before which Bakhita had frequently expressed her desire to enter religious life.

These points of reference and security were suddenly removed in 1902 when Bakhita was asked to transfer to the Canossian house in Schio on Via Fusinato. There her superior was Mother Margherita Bonotto, who in 1910 would invite Bakhita to tell her life story.

With regard to this transfer, a little-known testimony exists that was given by Mother Maria Cavaliere during the official beatification proceedings in Vicenza. Mother Maria first met Bakhita in 1932 and got to know her well when they lived in the same community for long stretches until 1946. During one of these periods, Mother Maria explains, "the Servant of God personally told me that the transfer from Venice to Schio was the wish of the patriarch Giuseppe Sarto. She was happy about this and kept saying: 'We are always in the house of the Lord.' "

[1] Insofar as was possible in an epoch when religious congregations in general took little interest in the cultural formation of semi-literate religious who came from humble backgrounds, especially if such formation was not explicitly requested.

How much value we should put in these words still remains to be confirmed. Bakhita made this remark thirty years after the fact. Yet what it demonstrates with all probability is the enduring esteem and affection that linked the three figures of Checchini, the future Saint Pius X, and the future Saint Josephine Bakhita.

With the exception of a few temporary changes of residence, Mother Josephine remained in Schio until her death. Here she was assigned the tasks of cooking, serving as sacristan, and answering the door—simple duties, even considering the fact that she could write little more than her name. She could speak with a certain facility but almost exclusively in the dialect of Veneto. Everybody remembered her throaty voice, but even more they recalled the feeling that even though she was African and black, anyone could speak easily and comfortably with her, as countrymen and good friends always do.

Not surprisingly, her popularity grew rapidly when she was given the role of portress, which afforded her constant contact with people. Whoever knocked on the convent door on Via Fusinato always received a kind word and a big smile. To the mothers with their babies, to workers, to the gardener, to those who knocked asking for directions or information, to each and every one Mother Josephine dispensed serenity and—whenever the time was right—human and spiritual advice. Her manner was so spontaneous and natural that, as all the testimonies affirmed, nobody was ever offended. This held true even in those cases when Bakhita chided a mother or a schoolgirl about dressing appropriately and wearing a modest amount of makeup.

As with writing, Bakhita also experienced difficulty with reading, so that the extent of what she read consisted almost exclusively of her prayer book and the Canossian Rule. These texts she practically knew by heart. Thus, over the course of her religious life, it would often happen that one of the sisters, a priest, or a visitor at the convent would find Bakhita in church absorbed in prayer. Afterward, they would ask her what she was praying or meditating about. Bakhita would invariably respond, "I was meditating on the life of Christ, so as to come to know him more and more, so as to love him"—and also so that others might come to know and love him, since she never let an opportunity slip by to tell Gospel stories to children and to the orphans who were taken care of in the convent.

Children fully understood and appreciated Bakhita's stories, which were always accompanied by many expressions of affection and devotion: "I believe that Bakhita exercised the Christian virtues in a heroic way, not so much because of anything unique or extraordinary she did, but rather because of the continuity, the naturalness, and the joy that permeated her day-to-day life", explained Armando Toniello, a longtime literature teacher at the high school in Schio, who as a young boy used to visit Mother Josephine from 1920 to 1923, when he served as an altar boy in the convent church. "I lived across the street from the convent," he recalled, "and Mother Bakhita, who was the sacristan, often asked me to help her on various liturgical occasions ... I was always struck by the way she handled the religious articles with such care, a sign of her deep faith and reverence for sacred things. It seemed as though her hands skimmed ever so reverently over the white linens."

Bakhita carried out her everyday tasks with the same kind of joy, attentiveness, and availability, as can be seen in this testimony from Sister Carlotta Fabruzzo:

102

Around 1907 Mother Bakhita was serving as head cook, and it was in this context that I witnessed her virtues ... In the kitchen her humility and charity were radiant. She tried to satisfy everyone's needs but particularly those of the sick and the elderly. I served as a nurse in the community, and when I requested something for the sick sisters that she had not prepared, she said with great humility, "Poor me, I have little memory; I'm sorry. I'll prepare it right away." If I saw she was very busy and told her not to worry about it, that I would prepare it myself, she would look at me with her beautiful eyes full of humble gratitude, join her hands together, and say to me, "Thank you, thank you, you are truly doing an act of charity for me."

Sister Anna Dalla Costa, who worked in the kitchen with Bakhita in 1911, spoke of

the tender care she offered so that sisters, orphans, and schoolgirls would feel happy; so that the sisters who ate their meals at the second sitting would find their food well prepared and arranged. In winter she would place bowls of soup in the oven so they would be warm for the sisters when they arrived. Other times she would cover the bowls with a plate.[2] When she would bring food to the nursery school, as soon as the children caught sight of her, they would cling to her habit and would not let go. There were five or six who absolutely refused to eat unless Mother Bakhita spoon-fed them. Oh, how they loved her!

Sister Giulia Campolongo, when she was already a missionary in India, wrote in a letter from 1957:

[2] For those who have the good fortune to dine with the sisters in the house at Schio, covering the soup is a very practical custom that has continued to this day.

We schoolgirls truly loved her. And we really liked her cooking. She prepared simple food, but it was full of flavor. Her fare was so well arranged on the plates and so clean that even the most finicky eaters were won over. In our simple, little-girl way, on feast days we would send our empty plates back to the kitchen with some little holy card for the Little Brown Mother as a sign of our affection and gratitude. From time to time we would ask her to join us and to tell us a story. And I remember that when she told us the most tragic parts, the calm and serene expression for which she was known always remained. She did not have enemies. Every suffering in her life was always a gift of the good Lord.

1915–1918: The field hospital

During the First World War, Schio found itself in a militarily strategic position. A short distance from the front lines (Mount Grappa is very visible from the city), Schio became a key reference point for the rearguard. In May 1916 the Canossian house at Schio was turned into a field hospital. A column of wounded soldiers arrived from the front. The military leaders asked the sisters for space, and they woke up all the children in the orphanage and the girls' school. Soon an evacuation operation was under way to the house in Mirano Veneto. A large number of sisters were sent to this other house. Bakhita remained in Schio (even though she could have gone to stay in Mirano, where she had well-known friends), with a few others, in order to continue serving as sacristan and cook. When she was able to do so, Bakhita aided the nurses and gave comfort to the wounded and dying soldiers.

Mother Genoveffa De Battisti remembered:

It was not a rare sight to have officers and soldiers standing around the Little Brown Mother, all wanting to hear her story. Bakhita, equipped with Mother Superior's permission, and with a simplicity that was all her own, narrated in her ungrammatical language the adventures and facts that she always attributed to the good God, who guided her with a special love to become his spouse. Who paid attention to her grammatical mistakes? Who laughed? Nobody. All of them were filled with admiration and compassion for that innocent one who had suffered so much and who appeared in their eyes to be an extraordinary being. And her lectures about eternal truths? More than one of her listeners would have taken them to heart, treasuring them later during the dangerous trials of war. And the reprimands she would give if she heard someone cursing? It did not matter if it came out of the mouth of a simple foot soldier or an officer—she would give them a warning and then made a point of exhorting and enlightening them about eternal truths until the guilty party promised to make amends and wanted to regain God's grace.

Bakhita worked as much as she could to help the wounded and dying. As soon as she completed her tasks as cook and sacristan, she would go to the hospital rooms to be of help, and when she could not provide physical assistance in the sick bay, she offered spiritual aid. Thus, while there are those who remembered how quick she was to give her own pillow to soldiers with cranial wounds, there are many others whose testimony underscored how much time she spent at the bedsides of those who were about to die and how she managed to reassure and comfort those who suffered the most atrocious pain. Sister Walburga Ricchieri recalled that "she showed the soldiers such tender care and attentiveness that she was able to comfort their very souls." A number of these soldiers, after recovering and returning to civilian life, continued writing letters to Bakhita for many years.

One of Saint Magdalene of Canossa's counsels comes to mind in this context. In what is considered her spiritual testament, the founder of the Canossians exhorts her sisters as follows: "I urge you more than ever, my beloved poor ones: strive to help everyone so that one day they may discover the joy of Christ through your teaching, prayers, love, and hard work."

There are numerous, if fragmentary, accounts of those who witnessed Bakhita at work ministering in the midst of the agonies of war, whether it be to a very young man or to a father of a family brought back from the trenches all torn to pieces in body as well as in spirit. We know how awful the wounds suffered in this conflict were, often as a result of unconventional warfare. We also have written works, based on firsthand testimonies, such as the novel *All Quiet on the Western Front*, that reveal how deeply consoling it was for the wounded, even in the face of extreme pain and the certainty of death, to find someone in the hospital who was capable of giving real solace and love. And Bakhita "had a particular art", said Sister Anna Dalla Costa, "for comforting and soothing the dying and those who were about to have an operation. It seemed as though she transfused all her strength and serenity into them." [3]

---

[3] The Capuchin priest Bartolomeo Cesaretti da Grotte di Castro, who was the chaplain of the military hospital on Via Fusinato, recalled that during this period Bakhita "served as sacristan and cook. She was humble and simple, held in high esteem, and treated with great respect by all the soldiers. Everyone had the sense that he was dealing with an extraordinary person. The medical staff often spoke with admiration of the African sister and about the way in which her work always radiated calmness, peace, and humility."

Mission years

In 1922 Bakhita contracted pneumonia. The illness was so grave that her sisters had the priest administer extreme unction. A few days later, however, Bakhita began to feel better. When the doctor announced that she was out of danger, she responded with words that stunned everyone: "What a shame! Since I was already leaving, it would have been better to continue on my way. Now I will have to start all over again." Once fully recovered, she was relieved of kitchen duty and was given less demanding work as portress and sacristan and helping in the refectory and wine cellar.

In 1927 Bakhita returned to Venice to make her perpetual vows. Two years later, in the same city, at the request of her superior, she had a number of meetings with Ida Zanolini, to whom she told the story of her life. The fruit of these meetings was the publication in 1931 of the biography *Tale of Wonder*, which achieved extraordinary success. It was then printed in several languages, receiving further acclaim. The annual number of visitors to Schio soon began to climb, for people wanted to speak with the Little Brown Mother, as she was called in the book. Similar requests multiplied from superiors of Canossian houses whose sisters, after reading *Tale of Wonder*, wanted Bakhita to come visit them so they could get to know her and make her known to others.

The only three well-known photographs of Bakhita that we have can be traced to this period.[4] These were taken by

---

[4] All in all, very few photographs exist of Bakhita, whether of her alone or in a group. All of the unpublished ones are kept in the Canossian archives and, in rare cases, in private collections. The images reproduced in this book are a selection.

a famous photographer who, after reading *Tale of Wonder*, wanted to meet Bakhita and felt compelled artistically and journalistically to document on film such a unique person. These photos were shot by Giovanni Bruner from Trent, who was also the photographer of the pontifical household.

It was in the context of this unexpected celebrity that in 1932 or 1933 Mother Bakhita was asked to work promoting the missions. Thus began a period of travel and frequent moves from one Canossian house to another throughout all of central and northern Italy, including Tuscany, the Marches region, and Rome.[5] Beginning in May 1933, her constant companion on these journeys was Sister Leopoldina Benetti, who was the same age as Bakhita and who had spent thirty-five tough years (1891–1927) in the Chinese missions, in southern Shensi Province.

These were trying days for the naturally shy and unassuming Bakhita, who was obliged to appear and speak in public. And the people who attended these gatherings—in piazzas, parish halls, schools, and convents—always came in great numbers. Everyone wanted to see the nun from Africa who had once been a slave. She accepted her popularity as a trial to be borne out of obedience, in service to a good cause.

To Sister Eugenia Cherti, whom Bakhita had known both as a schoolgirl in Schio and later as a Canossian, she confided in semidialect how much suffering she had endured in that undertaking, adding, "Let us hope that it is good for the

[5] She arrived in Rome in December 1936 together with the sisters who would open the first Canossian mission in Africa. Their destination was Addis Ababa, and on December 11 they were received by Benito Mussolini in the palace on Piazza Venezia. In the next days Bakhita and the other sisters managed to arrange a meeting with Pope Pius XI. This encounter made such an impression that on many subsequent occasions Bakhita insisted on the need to pray for the Holy Father, burdened by so much suffering that he had to endure because of those who did not love the Church.

missions, and especially for my family and my people. It does not matter if I see them here on earth, but to see them in heaven."

Another young nun, Mother Santina Baratto, had shared a room in Vicenza for some time with Mother Josephine during the period of her missionary journeys, and she recalled being struck because she often found Bakhita "on her knees, sighing and weeping". Mother Santina asked her on several occasions what the matter was yet received only elusive answers—until one day, since she was a nurse, she asked whether Bakhita felt ill and needed to see a doctor. At that point Mother Josephine opened her heart and revealed all the vexation she felt at being in the limelight and how this popularity seemed to be taking a heavy toll on her usual confidence in her dialogue with God and her serenity with others: "No physical suffering, no, but everyone looks at me like a nice beast. I want to work, to pray for everybody, and not to look at people. And they also say, 'Poor little thing, poor little thing.' But I am not a poor little thing, because I belong to the *Paròn* and I am in his house. Anyone who is not with the Lord, they are the poor ones."

With Sister Teresa Martini, who was very close to her during her final years, Mother Josephine shed further light on how ill at ease she felt with all the acclaim she received from people: "What a sacrifice! I felt like I was in danger ... too well liked, too loved ... Here I can now love the Lord alone."

Mother Benetti, the missionary to China, in a letter from 1947, shortly after Bakhita's death, writes:

My task was to give support to the late deceased, for she was unable to express herself with her simple dialect in front of the crowds that surrounded her and hemmed her in from all sides ... I kept her close to me at all times, and at the end of these meetings I would invite her to speak from the heart. Immediately she would stand up, and with her special gestures she would thank everyone and say goodbye to everyone, with assurances that she would remember them before God so that one day they might all meet again in heaven.

When she then stepped down from the stage, it was always a madhouse. Everyone would want to kiss her medal, hear her accent, have her sign *Tale of Wonder*, find out some unique little fact ... One nun was moved to write to me because she retained a strong impression of Bakhita's great humility. She said that she had encountered her at a number of Canossian houses, always surrounded by the people touching her and crossing themselves out of devotion and asking her to bless their babies and sick ones, and Bakhita did all of this with the greatest simplicity, as if it were the most natural thing in the world.

As if she were right there in front of you

The list of places Bakhita visited on her mission journeys is very long. Over the course of nearly four years she covered dozens of towns. Many were in the Veneto region, where the Canossians had a dense network of contacts. And then there were the big cities, such as Bologna, Ancona, Milan, Lodi, Florence, Modena, Venice, Padua, and Trent. The sites were so many and so far from one another that Mother Josephine, gazing one day at a map showing all the places and cities she had visited, could barely believe how much she had traveled.

At every meeting it was the sister accompanying Mother Josephine who spoke to the people about the missions and who presented Bakhita and her story. Then Bakhita would stand up and offer a few words, usually several phrases spoken haltingly (due to the various difficulties mentioned above). She did not say much, but because of the spiritual conviction behind her words and the sincerity they conveyed, she made a lasting impact. "I am here", she affirmed during the course of a meeting at the Canossian house in Venice, "because the *Paròn* has been so good to me. And he loves all of you. Love him in return, and do not offend him by sinning."

For her there was nothing else to say, and she spoke about the same things almost every time. After speaking, she quickly sat back down again, unless her companion or the people made her recount some episodes from her life in Africa and how she came to hear the gospel. Talking about her own life surely came much more easily and spontaneously when she visited schools, where her audience was made up mainly of children.

In this context, we have the beautiful recollection of the well-known exorcist Father Gabriele Amorth, who comes from the Emilia-Romagna region and who works in Rome.

It must have been around 1933. I was seven years old, and I was in first grade in the school run by the Sisters of Charity of Saint Giovanna Antida, on Via dei Servi in Modena. I remember it well, because only the first two grades were mixed. A black sister came, and for us it was something amazing. In Modena no one had ever seen a black person before. She told us her story. Her kidnapping, her escape with the other young girl, the lion that wanted to eat her, the tree in which she hid, how the lion went away, her liberation ... She understood well what children liked. I remember it as if it were yesterday ... She was a beautiful person. She spoke Italian well enough, or else we children could not have understood her.

I never saw her again, but I would often hear people talking about her. And at such times—like right now—I would remember how she looked ... and her somewhat awkward Italian. I also recall a book that told her story. Inside there were hand-drawn pictures and on the cover black arms with broken chains.

The bishop who shut the doors on Hitler

Monsignor Elia Dalla Costa, as archpriest and pastor of Schio, often celebrated Mass in the convent church on Via Fusinato. These were the years when Bakhita served as sacristan. Observing how she always cleaned and cared for the altar with such devotion and attention to detail, the monsignor affectionately dubbed her "Jesus' busy bee". A relationship of mutual sympathy grew between them. (Monsignor Elia took notice of Mother Josephine's extraordinary virtues, and later as a bishop and cardinal he made a point of publicly recognizing these qualities.) Part of the monsignor's sympathy may also have been related to the time he celebrated Mass for the first time in the Canossian convent, when he embarrassed himself in his initial encounter with the Sudanese nun.

This particular incident is but one of the many, often humorous occasions on which Bakhita's skin color elicited bewilderment in some people. In this circumstance, all the sisters were kneeling at the altar rail to receive Communion. As Monsignor Elia made his way down the line of nuns, he asked Mother Josephine to remove her veil, so that he could give her the Eucharist. Not receiving a reply, he repeated the request. At that point, the nun understood. Lifting her eyes to the priest and unveiling one of her brilliant smiles, Bakhita affirmed with perfect serenity, "I am black, Father."

This episode took place in the years immediately preceding the Great War. Born in Villaverla in the province of Vicenza in 1872 and ordained a priest in 1894, Monsignor Elia had just been appointed the parish priest of Schio, where he would remain during the entire conflict. Named bishop of Padua in 1923 and archbishop of Florence in 1931, he became a cardinal in 1933—that is, the same year Bakhita began her missionary trips. But these were also the years when the Fascist Party revealed the full force of its ruthless ideology. The cardinal lost no time in raising his voice in protest against the regime's pernicious policies. These public criticisms coincided with his implacable opposition to Nazism and its racist laws. When Hitler visited Florence at Mussolini's invitation, the cardinal—in open protest against the civil authorities' command that windows be decked out with flags and banners—ordered that all the windows and doors in the bishop's residence be shut tight. In the following years, especially during World War II, his top priority was to protect all those persecuted by Nazism and to prevent Florence from becoming a victim of reprisals and of the ravages of war.

A man of great human and moral depth, Cardinal Dalla Costa made a point of meeting with Bakhita when he heard about her arrival in Florence on behalf of the missions. Let us listen to the brief account of this encounter given by Sister Benetti in 1947, keeping in mind the idiom of the period and the somewhat self-important and maternalistic manner in which the nun spoke about Bakhita, almost as if she were the one introducing the Sudanese sister to the cardinal rather than vice versa: "In Florence I presented her to His Eminence the cardinal. He received us with great pleasure, also inviting into the parlor his venerable mother and his reverend secretary. We all engaged in amiable conversation. He then said to me: 'Oh, how Mother Bakhita worked and worked at Schio!'"

The long-lost sister

Sister Benetti's recollections make us realize how well known Bakhita already was during her own lifetime and how her humble charism struck a deep chord in the hearts of so many people she met.

In Bologna the two Canossian nuns also met the cardinal of that city. Mother Benetti recalled that he set aside other commitments just so he could have the opportunity to speak with the African nun. In Ancona it was the bishop himself who went out of his way to find Bakhita in the house where she was staying in Colle Ameno: "Not finding him in the residence when we went to visit him, Archbishop Giardini, to our great astonishment, drove up to Colle Ameno by car on the very next day. He then went through the park and came to the boarding school, where he waited for our dear Bakhita. He asked her many questions, and at the end he blessed her with many moving words."

So many people wanted to see Bakhita, observed the Canossian missionary with perhaps a note of exaggeration, that in several cities "even the trams came to a standstill because of the huge crowds ... In one church it was so packed—over four thousand people—that they wanted her up in the pulpit so they could see her better." On this same occasion, Bakhita expressed herself in her usual way: "Be good. Love the Lord. Pray for the unfortunate ones who do not know him. Know that it is a great grace to know God!"

During these trips around Italy, there were also moments of relaxation. We know, for instance, that when Mother

Bakhita traveled near Mirano or went to Padua she made a point of trying to visit Checchini's children and grandchildren.

One day Bakhita made an unusual discovery. In the cloister of the Visitation Sisters of Soresina, in the province of Cremona, there lived a Sudanese nun. Bakhita wanted to meet her and set out to do so. An emotional encounter took place. The stories of the two women bore such a resemblance that the two nuns, in recounting them to each other, clearly recognized the Lord's hand at work. In sharing their memories and feelings about having lost their families, they even came to the conclusion at a certain point that the two of them must be long-lost sisters.

The name of this sister was Maria Agostina. She was a few years older than Bakhita (about the same age as her kidnapped older sister). She, too, had been made a slave, and it had also been an Italian who ransomed her.[6] As an adolescent she was entrusted to the care of the Salesians of Soncino, and she subsequently decided to become a nun. She was more than eighty years old when she died, a short time before Bakhita's death.

The encounter between the two Sudanese nuns was recorded by Sister Benetti in this way:

The brief but joyful meeting between the little brown Visitation sister and the little brown Canossian nun was indescribable. Words cannot convey how much happiness dear Sister Maria Agostina felt in seeing good Mother Bakhita as her own dearest sister. She was completely convinced of this, and it seemed to me that Bakhita was too. I do not remember anything about what they said to one another,

[6] She was ransomed by Father Biagio Verri, who in the mid-nineteenth century founded the Association for the Redemption of Slaves, which was active in Africa for at least two decades.

except this: Sister Agostina, filled with joy and emotion, said, "Oh, how I thank the Lord for giving me this satisfaction", and her tears came streaming down. Bakhita replied, "We will see each other again." In fact, we are certain that they are already together again, in heaven.

This encounter was very similar to another one that took place between the 1920s and 1930s. Sister Carlotta Fabruzzo related that after having lived in Schio together with Bakhita for thirteen years, she was transferred to the Canossian house in Malamocco, near Venice, where elderly sisters or those in convalescence went during the summer months to take in the sun and sea air. Bakhita was also sent there, probably following her bad bout of pneumonia in 1922.

When I was transferred to the house in Malamocco, I still had occasion to see Bakhita because she came in the summer to take in the sun. I remember one time how she kept asking me if I could take her to Venice with me when I went there to get medical supplies. Her insistence surprised me, but then I came to realize her motive for wanting to make that journey. In Venice, at the Saint Lawrence Hospital, an old woman was being cared for who was not European, a woman by the name of Sarah with a dark olive face.[7] I do not know how Mother Josephine knew her. It is certain, however, that this soul who converted from paganism was very close to Bakhita's heart. She wanted to give her comfort and encouragement. When I was able to bring her there, I was extremely moved by the conversation between these two converted souls: they were simple words, but they gave forth a heavenly perfume. Later, in responding to the elderly woman as they bid each other farewell,

[7] Perhaps an old acquaintance from the period of the catechumens.

Bakhita kept on repeating, "We will see each other in paradise."

Will the planes bomb Schio?

Between 1936 and 1938 Mother Josephine resided for long stretches in the Vimercate house, near the Canossian novitiate for the foreign missions. There she served as portress. It is certain, however, that during this time she made several more trips on behalf of the missions. One of these was remembered by Sister Maria Luisa Dagnino, who in 1938 traveled with Bakhita and Sister Benetti to the city of Voghera.

In 1938 Mother Bakhita returned permanently to Schio. Ailments began to afflict her with greater frequency, and she walked with difficulty. In December 1943, on the occasion of her fiftieth anniversary of religious life, she was constrained to use a wheelchair.

During World War II, Bakhita became a reference point for mothers and wives who had children and whose husbands were at the front. Believing that Mother Josephine was a living saint, the people of Schio were convinced that their homes would be spared from the bombing raids. Bakhita herself, on more than one occasion, affirmed that the bombs would not fall upon houses. She remained utterly unfazed when the sirens sounded and bombers flew over the convent. Only once did bombs hit a building, a wing of the Rossi wool mill, killing fourteen workers. On another occasion, fifty bombs were dropped on the outskirts of Schio, yet none of them exploded. Over the course of the war, not a single house in the city was damaged—just as she had predicted.

"Little Brown Mother, will the planes bomb Schio?" the people asked. Bakhita invariably responded, "No, no. Do not worry; Schio will be saved." Then, on February 14, 1945, when four planes dropped sixteen bombs on the wool mill, the people returned in fear, asking, "Have you seen, Mother, that they came to Schio?" Bakhita explained, "Yes. And they will come again, but not to the houses. The homes will not be touched." And thus it was, even though the Allies bombarded the bridges and machine-gunned other targets. One day, the displacement of air caused by one of the numerous bombs knocked a seated baby right out of his house, yet he was not hurt, even though the drinking glass he was holding was shattered to bits.

In the middle of one air raid warning, the sisters rushed to Bakhita's room. They found her in her wheelchair and insisted on bringing her to the shelter with them. She was unperturbed: "No, no, the Lord who has saved me from lions and panthers—won't he save me from the bombs? In a little while the wheelbarrows[8] will go back home."

Between one alarm and the next, the people on the street would reply as follows to those wondering whether Schio would be bombed: "I have faith it won't, because in Schio we have the Little Brown Mother, and she is a saint!"

Then the day of the city's liberation arrived. The sisters celebrated like the rest of the inhabitants, but there were some who confided their misgivings and worries to Mother Josephine. As calm as ever, Bakhita simply said, "Pray and be good!" Then she invited to prudence those who were rejoicing too much that the hostilities were now over. "Unless there is more goodness, something worse will come to Schio." At the time she uttered these words, no one could imagine what was about to happen a short time later. What transpired in the summer of 1945, with the war officially

---

[8] *Carriole*: the term Bakhita used to describe military aircraft.

over, came to be called the "Schio Massacre". It was a tragic episode, to be numbered among the postwar vendettas. On the night between July 6 and 7, a group of ex-partisans killed fifty-four persons of all ages, including women and adolescents, accused of having been soldiers or sympathizers of the Italian Social Republic of Salò.[9]

Loosen the chains from me

We have seen that already in 1943 Bakhita sometimes used a wheelchair in order to move about. This became a necessity after she suffered an accidental fall, caused by a worsening of her old leg wounds. What deteriorated most significantly was the condition of her right thigh, which had been whipped and kicked by the slave trader's son in El Obeid. Then there were the respiratory problems linked to her 1922 battle with pneumonia that were aggravated by the winters in Schio, which are not exactly adapted to someone from sub-Saharan Africa. All of this, combined with the onset of circulatory and cardiac difficulties, forced her from 1945 on to spend a large part of her day in bed.

According to Massimino Bertoldi, the district municipal medical doctor of Schio and the doctor for the Canossian Sisters on Via Fusinato since 1927,

Mother Bakhita suffered from a degenerative myocardial condition leading to a progressive decline in function and low blood pressure. Ultimately, this condition led to acute pulmonary congestion, her immediate cause of death. I think that Mother Bakhita had previously experienced other

[9] The puppet state of Nazi Germany erected in 1943 and led by Benito Mussolini.—TRANS.

physical disturbances, even if minor, but she endured them on her own without speaking about them. My visits started to become frequent a year before her death. She also suffered from polyarthritis. Taking care of her body was not high on her list of priorities. Even at the end, it was her superior who took the initiative to inform me about her condition. With serene obedience she willingly accepted the medicines that were prescribed for her, indifferent to the remedy's outcome. She always endured her sufferings with patience, concerned solely with doing God's will. Whenever I asked her how she was feeling, she always replied, "As it pleases the Lord: it is he who is in charge."

The medical description is fairly straightforward, as is the manner in which Bakhita faced her illness and awaited the certainty of death. Among those who were able to visit or spend time with her regularly during this long period of suffering, nobody failed to be struck by how serenely she accepted her pain to the very last breath.

The testimonies in this regard are numerous, and we will present them later in the context of Mother Josephine's spirituality and virtues. At the end of this biographical chapter, it is enough to know that Bakhita's main concern during her illness, aside from constant prayer and the total offering of herself to God, was not to disturb anyone. At night, when she could no longer move her body without assistance, she never called the nurse but rather remained in the position in which she was left, suffering in silence so as not to inconvenience anyone. In response to a sister who delicately reproached her for not asking for help, Bakhita replied, "Why should I make someone who is sleeping lose sleep? I have plenty of time to rest later, while the day nurse has to work. Even if I suffer a little, what does it matter? I owe so much to the Lord that what I have to offer is nothing."

Let us revisit the last days of her life through the memories of a firsthand witness, Sister Anna Dalla Costa:

> Her heroic virtue stood out during her final illness. Never a complaint. Always content with everything and with everyone, grateful to those who cared for her, considering herself unworthy of so much care ... When in 1946 she became gravely ill and it was proposed that she receive the holy oil [extreme unction], she willingly said yes but affirmed that she was not going to die quite yet. In fact, she lived for nearly three more months.
>
> The last time the doctor visited her, always showing the utmost charity, he told her about his wife and son. After the doctor praised the beauty and strength of the child, Bakhita repeated: "Just as long as he grows up to be good", and then promised that she would pray for him.
>
> Before the doctor's arrival, a priest came who thought it was opportune to administer Communion. I then said to her, jokingly, "Would you like to receive Communion, Mother Bakhita, at this hour?" It was eleven o'clock in the morning. "Yes," she replied, "because later I will not be able to ... I'll be in paradise."

A perfect awareness of the moment of death is a characteristic many saints share. On at least two occasions, as we have seen, Bakhita demonstrated that she knew when she would die. In the same way, 112 years earlier, on the very day of her death, Saint Magdalene of Canossa revealed a similar awareness. Right after her doctor left the room, content with the saint's improved condition, Mother Magdalene, dismayed at the man's inability to discern the fragility of her situation, affirmed, "This blessed doctor will not let himself be persuaded that today I will die."

Let us return to Sister Dalla Costa's account.

In the afternoon, another priest came to bring her viaticum. He commended himself to her prayers, and she promised to pray for him, for the monsignor archpriest, and for all priests.

Toward evening she said, "These chains around my feet are so heavy." So I made as if I were taking them off, lifting up the covers. "That is enough", she told me. "Now it is time to go see Saint Peter." Thinking she was delirious and wanted to go to the local parish church,[10] I replied, "Yes, yes, the two of us are going very soon, arm in arm, and we will climb up the cathedral's long stairway." "No", she answered. "Not that Saint Peter but the one in paradise. I will introduce myself to him and ask him to call for our Lady." (In that moment she seemed to see her for real, and she smiled so beautifully that it made a lasting impression on me.) "Here, here", she continued. "Are you here? Come, come, let's go to the foundress.[11] Now, when I am there I will not go away anymore, and I will stay there forever."

These were her last words. A few seconds later, after a loud death rattle, she expired.[12]

I will not frighten anyone, and I will pray for you

Bakhita died on the evening of February 8, 1947. "After I die, I will not frighten anyone ... When I am in heaven I will pray for everyone", she had said on several occasions during her final months. And so it happened, in a series of

[10] The cathedral parish of Schio is dedicated to Saint Peter.

[11] Magdalene of Canossa.

[12] The same sister also provided a slightly more extensive version of Bakhita's last moments, which rounds out the statement "These were her last words." Sister Dalla Costa said, "During the final moments I suggested to her the ejaculations "Jesus", "Joseph", "Mary". I encouraged her to repeat them. At a certain point, uttering the words 'in my agony', she raised her head and eyes to heaven, with the hint of a sweet and serene smile. Then she retreated into herself and expired."

extraordinary events that many found astonishing, first of all the medical personnel and sisters who bathed and dressed her for her final journey. In particular, they were stunned and profoundly moved at the sight of the 114 tattoo wounds that covered her body, as well as of the deep, hollowed-out part of her right thigh caused by the whipping she had suffered.

The crowds that came streaming to her room of repose (situated more or less where the saint's remains are preserved today) were endless. Hundreds of children stood before her exposed corpse, showing no signs of fear but, instead, looking upon her with awe and amazement, caressing her and laying their heads gently against the hands of the deceased nun, whose body remained incredibly soft and warm.

Almost immediately the graces and miracles began to flow. Three years later, the missionary bulletin of the Canossians, *Vita* (Life), issued a six-page list with the names of people who had received graces and had had their prayers answered in the years 1947, 1948, and 1949.

The first such grace that we know about involves a man who had been without work for some time, unable to bring home enough income for his family. Bakhita's corpse had just been placed in the room of repose. He entered, removed his hat, and began to speak almost out loud, begging Bakhita to help him find work because he had nowhere else to turn. After a while he put his hat back on, left the room, and went to the Rossi wool mill. Here he apparently spoke with the right person—a few hours after uttering his prayer, he was given a job.

Several days later, a student at the Canossian girls' school in Schio who was studying to be a garment worker was brought to the hospital, where her little toe was amputated due to an infection caused by chilblains. However, the infection kept getting worse. Her leg swelled up, and the doctors prepared to amputate the leg. The night before the operation, her friends prayed to Bakhita, slipping a little picture of the nun along with a piece of her clothing inside the folds of the girl's foot bandages. In the morning, when the bandages were removed, the doctors discovered that they were saturated with pus. Then they observed only a small discharge from the place where the toe had been amputated. A few days passed, and the girl was completely healed.

Later we will speak more at length about the long list of miracles and graces received, in particular when we consider the official miracles, namely, those that accorded Mother Josephine the honor of being raised to the altars. Here we will report a third account so as to highlight how quickly the manifestation of graces followed upon Bakhita's death. In June 1947, the bulletin *Vita* published a letter by the sister of a Canossian nun dated May 21. The text, slightly disjointed, tells the story of the unexpected return home of two veterans from the Russian front. The joyful news that this woman shares with her sister is that the two veterans are her very own son and husband: "Finally, after six years, I received a letter from my son Romeo. I also thank you, Lord and our Lady, who, through the intercession of Mother Bakhita, granted me this grace. The letter arrived right when they had notified me that he was dead. And it arrived on the same day as Alfred's letter! They were both dated February 8, the day Bakhita flew to heaven. How much I have prayed to her!"

Schio kneels before its saint

When Bakhita died, the little town in Italy's Veneto region, where she had lived for over fifty years, came to a standstill.

Even though the weather was inclement, the snow and ice did not deter the people in the least. In front of the door of the house on Via Fusinato that led up to the room of repose, people formed a line that kept getting longer and longer. All the people who had known Bakhita or had at least glimpsed her once joined the line. As the hours passed, people from the surrounding villages started to come, then from the nearby cities. Entire families that had heard about her or read about her in *Tale of Wonder* come to Schio. So many people arrived that the sisters were forced to regulate the flow of visitors, having them enter in groups. And those who left then attracted others, telling them about what everybody was calling a miracle: the suppleness of the African nun's body, the pink color of her lips. She did not seem dead but merely asleep.

The following account comes from the testimony given by Mother Fabruzzo during the beatification process.

Mother Bakhita's corpse retained its natural beauty—it was composed and flexible, with red lips as if she were alive—until the moment the casket was closed, that is, on the day of February 11. Mother Antonietta Filippin told me that she had felt her limbs warm fifteen hours after she died ... She died on Saturday evening, and the next day the monsignor, archpriest of Schio, along with the other priests from the parish and other churches announced the news to the people ... The corpse was visited by tremendous crowds—people of every class, age, and condition. The workers from Lanificio Rossi, the wool mill, telephoned the Canossians, and on Monday evening they all arrived,[13] giving homage

[13] On late Monday afternoon the casket was about to be sealed when there was a phone call from the wool mill. The decision was made to postpone the sealing of the casket until the workers had made their visit.

with great respect to the one whom they called "Mother". The funeral was held in Schio's parish church [the cathedral] on Tuesday, February 11 ...[14] The coffin was carried on the shoulders of the young men from the Canossian workshop. The procession that followed was one mile long ... She was buried in Schio's cemetery. A competition of sorts took place in order to prevent Mother Bakhita's remains from being buried in the ground. Mrs. Gasparella[15] received the privilege of interring the corpse in her family vault and of providing the expenses of a double casket ... On the gravestone are inscribed these words: "Born in Africa in 1869—died in Schio 8-2-1947. Mother Josephine Bakhita, Canossian. Here lie her brown remains; heaven holds her white soul. Daughter of the African desert, granted the honor to be a spouse of Christ, in the glory of the just she speaks to the good Lord on our behalf."

Schio's parish bulletin, *Flame of the Sacred Heart*, in the issue for February 1947, noted the following: "The innumerable visitors were very moved and filled with esteem as they beheld the smiling composure of the deceased. Even two days after death, her limbs displayed none of the rigidity of death but rather preserved a surprising softness and elasticity."

"Even the doctors", we read in the pages of the Canossian bulletin *Vita* from April 1947, "expressed their amazement, observing how the corpse retained its flexibility, soft flesh, and pink lips." These extraordinary findings only increased Bakhita's already-established reputation of

[14] The funeral Mass was celebrated by the archpriest of the cathedral, Gerolamo Tagliaferro.

[15] Mrs. Gasparella's husband had been unjustly incarcerated several years earlier but was able to prove his innocence with the aid of Bakhita's prayers.

sanctity.[16] Sister Martini, superior of the Schio house, writes in one letter:

It was truly a procession inspired by the people. Men, women, and children came to see our dear one, and they asked for images, which they left for a moment in the hands of Mother Bakhita, or they asked for a little piece of her clothing. They handed objects that they were carrying or wearing (necklaces, wristwatches, fountain pens) to the sisters who were keeping vigil near her corpse, that they might be blessed by touching Bakhita's hands. They presented their wedding rings and wanted them placed on her fingers. At certain moments, the hands of the deceased were literally covered with golden rings, which stood out against her black skin, and then they were quickly given back to their devoted owners.

Antonia Munari, sister of Father Giovanni (whom we will introduce shortly), lived on Via Fusinato as a child, next door to the Canossian convent. When Bakhita died, Antonia was sixteen years old. Today she still remembers vividly the time when she, like everyone else, went to view the deceased nun. She could barely contain herself when she recalled the experience:

I was afraid of dead people. I approached very slowly, circling the corpse in the line. Everyone was carrying something to touch to her body, and there were others who

[16] In *Vita*'s issue for April 1947, we also read: "Numerous visitors declared that they had never wanted to see dead people, not even relatives, but they were drawn to Mother Bakhita. Certain mothers even desired that one of her hands be placed as a blessing upon the heads of their children, which did not disturb them at all. By the evening of the tenth day, people had made off with nearly half of her clothing."

would cut off a little piece of her clothing or a curl of her hair that came out from under her veil. The nun who was next to me, who knew me, asked if I also had something to place on Bakhita's body. "I don't have anything", I replied, and the nun then suggested that I use my watch. Then the line ended, and I went up to Mother Bakhita, placing it in her hand. The nun closed her hand, opened it again, and then gave me back the watch. I stood there like a stone. I thought that the soft limbs after death must be a phenomenon associated with black people . . . I still have that watch. A few years ago I left it with a mother who had a handicapped child who could not even stand. She returned it to me after a couple of years. Now that little girl can walk and is able to go to nursery school . . . In the room of repose my mother took a snippet of Bakhita's clothing. Years later, when I was visiting her in the hospital because of her acute diabetes, I noticed outside of her door a woman who was crying for her dying husband. I gave her this relic, counseling her to put it under his pillow. The next day, I saw that she was happy. Her husband had awakened from a coma, saying, "I felt someone place something under my pillow, and I got better."

Escrivá and Bakhita: Saints promoting sanctity

From 1953 to 1955 an information-gathering process took place in the province of Vicenza. Then from 1968 to 1969 an apostolic process occurred. The body of Mother Josephine Bakhita was exhumed and transferred from the local cemetery to the house on Via Fusinato.

On December 1, 1978, Pope John Paul II signed the decree confirming the heroic virtue of the Servant of God. On July 6, 1991, the beatification decree was promulgated. On May 17, 1992, she was beatified together with Josemaría

Escrivá de Balaguer, according to the express wish of the Pope. This pairing of saints, so to speak, perplexed those who had been following the beatification process of Mother Josephine. Even today, Monsignor Antonio Casieri, who at the time was a member of the Congregation for the Causes of Saints, remembered that many judged it a risky move to bring the two beatifications together. The fear was that the great and universally known founder of Opus Dei would completely overshadow the elevation to the altars of the unknown African ex-slave.

But instead, something extraordinary took place. The monsignor of noble origins and famous throughout the world, whose disciples on the day of his beatification filled Saint Peter's Square, opened up a "passageway" for Bakhita and made her known to the world. The crowd that gathered in Rome that day from all continents (250,000 pilgrims) were almost all present because of him. Yet Bakhita achieved another one of her "miracles of humility". Her story entered into the hearts of the people of Opus Dei, and these hearts carried her back to their countries. In this way, without anyone organizing a campaign to "promote" her "image" (if we may use these publicity terms for a moment), Bakhita reached the most remote places on the planet as well as the most populated cities.

John Paul II: A special love

How people of all social and racial strata were so powerfully able to recognize the holiness of this humble black woman can be understood in part from the account above, and we will return to this phenomenon later in greater depth. Even Pope John Paul II revealed a particular fondness for this saint, who was able to stir the crowds even though they had never heard her speak a single word.

It is a fondness that is easy to understand if one considers Karol Wojtyła's particular devotion to another humble nun, the Polish Faustina Kowalska, who was canonized on April 30, 2000. Born in 1905 into a poor peasant family from the village of Głogowiec, she worked as a housemaid for a wealthy family; in 1925, she entered the Warsaw convent of the Sisters of Our Lady of Mercy. She too carried out the most humble tasks as cook, gardener, and portress. She died in 1938 at the age of thirty-three in Kraków. The depth and power of her spirituality and mysticism emerged in her diary, written at the request of her spiritual director. It is through this diary, which has been translated into almost all languages, that devotion to Sister Faustina spread throughout the world, appealing widely to poor people and astonishing theologians by the profundity of thought coming from an uneducated nun. One of the first to be attracted to this figure was Wojtyła, who during his seminary studies often went to pray in the convent chapel in Kraków and who in 1965 as bishop initiated the process for her beatification.

Turning to John Paul II and Bakhita, we now present several key passages about Bakhita, drawn from the Pope's homily on the day of her beatification.

In Blessed Josephine Bakhita we have an eminent witness of God's fatherly love and a luminous sign of the perennial modernness of the Beatitudes.

In our time, in which the unbridled race for power, money, and pleasure is the cause of so much distrust, violence, and loneliness, Sister Bakhita has been given to us once more by the Lord as a universal sister, so that she can reveal to us the secret of true happiness: the Beatitudes.

Hers is a message of heroic goodness modeled on the goodness of the heavenly Father. She has left us a witness of evangelical reconciliation and forgiveness, which will surely bring consolation to the Christians of her homeland, the Sudan, so sorely tried by a conflict that has lasted many years and reaped so many victims. Their fidelity and their hope are a source of pride and thanksgiving for the whole Church. At this time of great trials, Sister Bakhita goes before them on the path of the imitation of Christ, of the deepening of Christian life, and of unshakable attachment to the Church.

At this juncture the Pope's words become "a heartfelt appeal to those who control the destiny of the Sudan", reminding them of their promises "of peace and harmony" so that "respect for fundamental human rights, and in the first place the right to religious freedom, will be ensured for everyone, without ethnic or religious discrimination". A second appeal is addressed to international aid organizations, that "they [may] continue to send their timely and urgently needed assistance" to the "hundreds of thousands of refugees from the South" who are forced to flee from civil war that has lasted decades. "Theirs is a tragic situation, and it cannot leave us unmoved", he says in reference to "the beloved people of the Sudan, always present in my heart", a people whom he entrusts "to the intercession of Blessed Josephine Bakhita".

He then continues, turning to the holiness of the two blesseds:

"A new commandment I give to you, that you love one another, even as I have loved you, that you also love one another. By this all men will know that you are my disciples, if you have love for one another" (Jn 13:34–35). With these words of Jesus, the Gospel of today's Mass ends. In this saying we find the summing up of all holiness, the holiness that Josemaría Escrivá de Balaguer and Josephine Bakhita attained, by paths that were different and yet that met at one and the same goal. They loved God with all the strength of their heart and gave proof of a charity taken to the point of heroism through their works of service to their brothers and sisters.

The next day, John Paul II welcomed to the Vatican the pilgrims who had come for Bakhita's beatification (many of whom were from Sudan, accompanied by their bishops and priests). The Pope offered words of greeting and recalled several episodes from the life of the saint, reminding them that "the example of Blessed Josephine Bakhita speaks of the difficulties and sufferings that continue to be so much a part of Sudan's history. Today her luminous example speaks to her brothers and sisters of the Church in the Sudan about the courage of faith and the power of evangelical love in the face of intense distress. Blessed Josephine Bakhita's life points to the victory of God's love over the ravages of sin and evil. It presents a striking example of the role of reconciliation in Christian life and practice."

Return to Africa

The penultimate act in this extraordinary journey into people's hearts and to the altars for the conversion of souls took place on February 10, 1993. This was the date of Bakhita's return to her native land, 124 years after her birth in the little village at the foot of a sandy hill in the heart of Africa.

On that day Pope John Paul II accompanied the relics of Mother Bakhita, bringing them back to Sudan in person, on the occasion of an official visit to Khartoum. From that moment, as we will see afterward, the history of Sudan bore within it a seed destined to change its course in ways and times that still remain unknown, even if we are already catching glimpses of new and wonderful realities on the horizon.

In Khartoum the people's welcome was among the most effusive that this Pope ever received, or would receive again, in Africa. Beyond the obvious differences in culture and geographical distance, there was something in the air reminiscent of John Paul II's first visit to Poland. A multitude of people composed of Catholics from all corners of the huge country, a large portion of whom were refugees from the South, were accommodated in the fields around the capital and its periphery as well as near the cathedral of Juba. Vast crowds numbering three hundred thousand persons lined up along the roads from the airport to the city. Later they flocked to the immense Green Square, the regime's military parade ground, where beside a large iron figure of Christ and an enormous image of Bakhita the Pope celebrated an open-air Mass. It was a liturgical event of tremendous spiritual as well as political import. It represented the official return of Bakhita to her people, the first Sudanese saint. It was also the first papal Mass in a country where *sharia* (Islamic law) was in force.

The people understood very well the dual meaning of the Pope's visit. They gave witness to their faith and to their suffering by bearing images of the Pope and their saint and with banners invoking liberty: "Pope, give us hope"; "Speak also for those who cannot speak"; "God created all men equal."

At the altar John Paul II was presented with a gift from the mother general of the Canossians, Sister Elide Testa:[17]

---

[17] During those days, the Daughters of Charity opened a new house in El Obeid with a school for the advancement of women.

a bronze reliquary bust of Mother Bakhita, which passed into the hands of the archbishop of Khartoum, Zubeir Waco. This gesture was accompanied by jubilant roars from the crowd. Then, in his homily, addressed to the multitudes before him, the Pope spoke in praise of the saint. The most moving and meaningful passages were met with interminable applause.

"Bakhita", John Paul II affirmed, "learned from the tragic events of her life to have complete trust in the Almighty, who is always and everywhere present ... To use religion as an excuse for injustice and violence is a terrible abuse, and it must be condemned by all true believers in God."

When it was nearly nightfall and the Mass was ended, the Holy Father extended to those who were present a final word: "Before I leave you I wish once more to encourage you to place your trust in God and not to lose heart, especially the young people who are the hope of a better future."

An hour or so later, at the airport before leaving for Italy, after parting words of farewell from the Sudanese president Omar Hassan Ahmed al-Bashir, the Pope said good-bye to Africa with a speech that sounded like an out-and-out revitalization program. In his words it is not difficult to detect the direct influence and example of Bakhita:

Yes! Africa is changing. Not at the same pace everywhere, and not always in the same direction. But it is clear that the peoples of Africa are expressing a new sense of responsibility for their own destiny ... Africa, you have such great needs, but you also have so much to give! You have a deep sense of community and a vivid sense of the spiritual dimension of human life. Do not be led to think that an exaggerated individualism, which always ends in selfishness, is the right way forward. Maintain the strength of your family

life, your love for children, your solidarity with those in
need, your hospitality toward the stranger, the positive ele-
ments of your social and cultural traditions. Above all, do
not exchange your spiritual values for a materialism that
cannot satisfy the human heart ... As I leave I express the
hope that the path of understanding and dialogue will soon
lead to a just and honorable peace ... I came to Khartoum
with friendship and esteem ... I depart with the hope that
a better relationship between North and South and between
the followers of different religious traditions will soon be a
reality ... God bless the Sudan!"

V

A Saint among Saints

A beloved daughter of God

In Bakhita holiness did not appear after a lengthy period of growth as was the case with other saints. Bakhita's story gives the impression that she was a saint from the moment she was abducted by the two Arab kidnappers. Reading her story one quickly senses the certainty of being in the presence of someone predestined, "guided by God".

This sense is confirmed by the testimony of Sister Teresa Martini during the beatification proceedings: "Mother Bakhita told me that as a slave she never despaired and that she felt within her a mysterious power that sustained her. As soon as Illuminato Checchini spoke to her about God, she saw a new horizon open up before her that she had glimpsed already but that she could not understand."

Nevertheless, as Bakhita attested on more than one occasion, as a child she did not know the Christian God or any analogous divinity (her family was animist), and she did not even have an idea of what a structured religion could be. She had simply been educated in the love of her family and in a general respect for nature and human beings.

One of Bakhita's best-known quotes recounts her experience when she still lived in her village. She would observe the sky at night, the sun in the morning, and all the other natural phenomena. Filled with wonder, she would ask herself, "Who could possibly be the master of these beautiful things? And I felt a great desire to see him, to know him, and to give him homage."

To Sister Eugenia Cherti, who lived in Schio from 1923 to 1929 and who asked about Bakhita's faith when she was in Africa, Mother Josephine denied ever adoring idols. Speaking candidly in the dialect of Veneto, she said, "In the morning I watched the sun as it was born and in the evening as it set. And I thought that if it was beautiful, how much more beautiful must be the one who had made it."

It is not hard to hear in these words powerful echoes of Saint Augustine (a classic example of holiness that developed over time), whose observations of nature provided him with a confirmation of God's goodness and love for man. In his *Confessions*, Augustine writes:

> See, heaven and earth are before our eyes. The very fact that they are there proclaims that they were created . . . Created things also proclaim that they did not create themselves . . . It is you, then, O Lord, who made them. You are beautiful, and they too are beautiful. You are good, and they too are good. You ARE, and they too are. But they are not beautiful and good as you are beautiful and good, nor do they have their being as you, their Creator, have your being . . . This I know, and thanks be to you for this knowledge. But our knowledge, compared with yours, is ignorance. (book 11, chapter 4)

Augustine's overall argument is more complex than Bakhita's intuitive conclusion, but the principle behind them is the same, as is the matter-of-factness with which God's sovereignty over all things is proclaimed. In terms of one's intimate knowledge of God, the learned saint and Church Father was no different from the illiterate saint who could barely write her name.

The complete confidence in God was shared by both of them.

At the beginning of chapter 12 in the *Confessions*, Augustine writes: "We have your promise, which none can make null and void. 'If God is for us, who can be against us' (Rom 8:31). 'Ask and you shall receive, seek and you shall find, knock and the door shall be opened to you' (Mt 7:7–8) ... These are your promises, and who need fear to be deceived by the promises of Truth himself?"

Almost as if responding to these lines, Mother Bakhita explained, "I give everything to the *Paròn*, and he takes care of me; he is obliged to." Later, near the very end of her life, with utmost devotion she affirmed, "Every moment I feel that death takes something away ... The Lord takes back what is his, and I am content to do what he wants."

A saint in the eyes of the people

One of the characteristics of Bakhita's holiness, perhaps the most attractive one, is that from the very start of her time in Schio the people who met her or had a chance to speak with her went away joyfully convinced that they had spoken with a saint. And this happened not only with the inhabitants of Schio, with whom at a certain point she developed relationships of mutual affection, but also with the other sisters, with the young students lodging at the Canossian house, with the priests who came to say Mass, with bishops who visited, and with those who, whether religious or lay, encountered Bakhita in her numerous journeys on behalf of the missions. A reputation of sanctity developed around her even before the book by Ida Zanolini brought her fame, both in Italy and abroad.

Sister Martini recalled that at the house in Schio, whenever spiritual exercises were offered for various groups of people, at the end Bakhita would always stop and talk with the guests, above all with the young women and little girls. "I always noticed how attentive these girls were to the words she spoke to them, at times being moved to tears. Many times, when she was ill and they knew she would be brought to church in her wheelchair, they waited for her to pass by in order to receive a word from her. I asked why they did that, and they replied that it was because Mother Bakhita is a saint."

In the diary of Giovanna Santulin, an orphan who was welcomed into the house at Schio in the 1920s, we find these words: "We all loved the Little Brown Mother a lot, and we said she was a saint. We did everything we could to get a glimpse of her. We even climbed up to peek through the windows of the sisters' dining room."

This sort of behavior was due in part to the curiosity that resulted from having a black person living in the house. Adding to the attraction was the fact that Bakhita was always friendly and smiling and also a little bit awkward at times. Nonetheless, it is evident that Bakhita had an uncanny ability to transform situations that most people would consider obstacles into opportunities to spread the love of God, which in turn became occasions for her magnetic holiness to shine through. Another graduate of the Canossian school, Aurelia Fuoli, underscored this point with clarity: "Whoever went to see her out of admiration or curiosity came away won over by her goodness."

The Franciscan father Bartolomeo, chaplain of the military hospital, recalled distinctly, "She was humble and simple. Everyone thought that this was an extraordinary soul.

In all the religious services, she was edifying to the sisters and whoever had the opportunity to see her." Ida Zanolini, a firsthand witness present at a meeting in Castenedolo for the foreign missions, said that "she was able to move the crowd deeply, urging the people to love the Lord ... The nun from the missions could give a speech, but everyone was straining to see Bakhita. Even those who were not practicing their faith were struck by her presence. I have been told that this happened wherever Bakhita went."

In the final months of her life, those who met her could sense that they were unquestionably in the presence of a saint. Mother Martini, the superior, repeatedly remarked upon this fact, and not only during the beatification proceedings: "Once you entered her room, you did not ever want to leave, so inviting and attractive was Mother Josephine."

It was a phenomenon that the bishop of Vicenza also found astounding. On March 31, 1946, while on a pastoral visit in Schio, Monsignor Carlo Zinato stopped in at the Canossian house, pausing several minutes to see Bakhita, who was ill. The mother superior and her assistant accompanied him from the front door to Bakhita's room. Sister Maria Cavaliere was the assistant superior, and a few days after this visit, she reported that as he came out of Bakhita's cell after conversing with her briefly, the bishop turned to the sisters who were present and exclaimed, "That is one holy religious!" Then, turning to the sisters after a moment, as Mother Antonietta Filippin recalled, the bishop added, "You are fortunate to have a saint in your midst."

Bakhita's general reputation for sanctity "was due to her objective holiness and extraordinary goodness", affirmed Sister Filippin. "When you were near her you understood that there was something extraordinary about her." Bakhita prayed constantly for the grace of holiness, and she also asked others to pray that she might be holy. In this context, an interesting episode was recounted during the official proceedings by Sister Ida Peripolli. One day, when young Ida was an adolescent at the girls' school in Schio, she was in the church when Bakhita asked her to run a little errand for her. Upon Ida's return, Bakhita had her come kneel down next to her in front of the tabernacle and said, "I will pray for you that the Lord may give you light for your choice in life, and you pray for me that the Lord may help me to be a holy nun."

Father Pietro Nichele, who taught catechism to the children at the Canossian house in Schio from 1937 to 1944, claimed that Bakhita "lived and breathed her faith and had a sense of dignity and gentleness that was attractive to all ... Everything she did made one think that she had reached a high level of virtue. When people told me that they had asked Mother Bakhita to pray for them, I replied that they did well to do so."

And Father Giuseppe Barban, assistant pastor in Schio from 1918 to 1932, added, "It was evident that she had supernatural faith. It was enough to watch how she prayed and comported herself in church—the way she genuflected, the way she made the sign of the cross. How she smiled after every visit to the chapel. Everything pointed to a profound and intimate union with God."

"Modern man", writes Pope Paul VI in *Evangelii nuntiandi*, "listens more willingly to witnesses than to teachers, and if he does listen to teachers, it is because they are witnesses."

Pius X, Magdalene, Comboni, and Escrivá

Pope Pius X, Magdalene of Canossa, Daniel Comboni, and Josemaría Escrivá are four saints whose lives are interwoven in the fabric of Bakhita's human and spiritual journey. Each one of these great figures followed a unique path, yet each one played a fundamental role in making Bakhita's charism and holiness known to the world.

Only with Pius X was there a direct acquaintance, which we have amply documented above. Giuseppe Sarto, after all, was the man who, in his capacity as patriarch of Venice, personally recognized Bakhita's great faith and her vocation, inviting her to consider the religious life.

Magdalene's life, on the other hand, fell exactly one century before Bakhita's, while that of Escrivá de Balaguer, which in part coincided chronologically with the life of the African saint, unfolded in a vastly different environment. Bakhita did not meet Comboni, either, even though for a brief time the Italian missionary (who died in Khartoum in 1881) and the young slave lived only a short distance from each other.

Let us first look at Daniel Comboni, whom we have just mentioned. In 1872 he founded a mission in El Obeid that was very active during the time Bakhita lived as a slave in the Turkish general's house, right there in Kordofan's capital between 1878 and approximately 1881–1882. The mission was destroyed in January 1883 when the Mahdi troops overtook El Obeid.

From 1879 to 1880 Comboni was in Italy, in part because of his responsibilities in running his fledgling congregation and in part because he was recuperating from a fever that had debilitated him. (From 1877 to 1879, northern Sudan was devastated first by drought, then by famine, and finally by a nearly unstoppable epidemic of typhoid fever that killed numerous Comboni missionaries and nuns.) While in Italy Comboni also was advocating the cause for beatification of Magdalene of Canossa.

Comboni had founded his religious congregation in Verona with the help of the city's bishop, Luigi Cardinal di Canossa, Magdalene's nephew. So when Comboni went to Rome in September 1879, summoned by Monsignor Charles Lavigerie to discuss the missions in the Great Lakes zone [in east central Africa], he also carried out an important task there for Cardinal Canossa. The latter was keenly interested in the cause of beatification of Magdalene, who died in 1853 and who was the foundress, in Verona, of the religious order the Daughters of Charity. Seeking an update about the status of the cause, Comboni went to the Congregation of Rites, which at the time was in charge of the causes of saints, and he received assurances from a prelate there that the Canossa file was making great headway. In reality, Magdalene's beatification would have to wait until 1941, during the pontificate of Pius XII.

The relationship between Bakhita and Bishop Comboni began from a distance. Their spiritualities were quite different. They were both ablaze with love for God and with charity for their neighbor. However, while the African nun's humble and hidden prayer life was her chief mode of evangelization, the bishop was above all a man of action, a dynamo of such apostolic zeal and energy that only sickness or death could slow him down.

In *Un profeta dell'Africa* [A prophet for Africa], Domenico Agasso writes: "Comboni practiced brotherhood also through what he criticized. He did not go to Africa as a benefactor visiting a nursery school; he was not a do-gooding philanthropist, all smiles and permissiveness. He wanted to eradicate an age-old scandal and believed Africans were the ones who needed to do it ... Within a relationship of total respect and fraternity he demands honesty above all else ... He railed against the fatalism of certain Africans in order to help them overcome it, to convince them that they were capable of doing it, provided they had the will to do so." To achieve this objective, Comboni was prepared to pour himself out to the very last drop.[1]

People began connecting Bakhita and Comboni in the 1950s and 1960s—a connection surely destined to ignite a new hope for the future in Africa. The first visible signs of this connection can be found in the cathedral of El Obeid. The large fresco behind the altar features Our Lady Queen of Africa bearing in her arms the Child Jesus, surrounded by jubilant angels. At her feet kneels Comboni, who seems to be presenting all of Africa to Jesus and Mary. On the right, wearing the Canossian habit, a young Bakhita prays intently on her knees with joined hands (as many witnesses have attested was her custom) for Africa and the African people. Both of these figures are depicted within the hilly, semidesert landscape of Kordofan.

This striking masterpiece was painted by a Russian Comboni nun who in the 1960s was asked to come to El Obeid in order to paint some angels around the Madonna and Child. Once the angels were added, however, it became clear that the work still remained incomplete. In the three days that remained at the nun's disposal, she included the figures of Comboni and Bakhita, inserting them within the landscape characteristic of Kordofan.

From then on, in Sudan and in many other African countries, Bakhita began to appear next to Comboni in paintings commissioned for churches and the missions. They were depicted in the same way as in El Obeid: Comboni presenting

---

[1] "I perform the work of a bishop, pastor, superior, priest, doctor, nurse, and gravedigger", wrote Daniel Comboni to an Italian friend in September 1878, when fevers and "fulminating typhus", as he called it, had decimated the religious brothers and sisters in his Sudanese missions.

Africa and Bakhita praying for its salvation. "In many chapels," explained Father Giuseppe Ramanzini, a Comboni missionary who had always worked in Khartoum, "you can find images of both Comboni and Bakhita, and during celebrations, as in everyday life, Comboni and Bakhita are always mentioned in the same breath together."

Maria Lucia Tokoyo, a Comboni nun from Congo, recalled that during Comboni's beatification celebrations holy cards were printed that featured the Italian bishop walking hand in hand with an African toward the Madonna and Child, with Bakhita praying beside them. "For African Christians," the nun emphasized, "Comboni represents the father who leads them to the faith and teaches that Africa can walk on its own two feet. Bakhita, meanwhile, is the proof that this is possible: an African—and, what is more, a woman—who is capable of being a role model for mankind." The witness of this saintly duo is also manifested on the African continent in an even more coordinated collaboration between Comboni and Canossian missionaries.

A very different kind of bond unites Josemaría Escrivá de Balaguer and Bakhita. It is a bond that, as we have already seen, was born on the day of their joint beatification in 1992. This dovetailing is said to have been strongly (one might even say prophetically) desired by Pope John Paul II, and it has continued to bear much fruit. It seems as though Escrivá bent down and took the humble nun by the hand, so that they both might go forth into the world together. And thus it happened, in a unique miracle of providence. Bakhita the African returned to Africa with the help of Comboni, and she reached the other continents thanks to the 250,000 members of Opus Dei who filled Saint Peter's Square on the beatification day and heard the Pope speak of Bakhita as our "universal sister"—the slave who in a world of hatred and wars was able to thank the slave traders who had kidnapped her and abused her; the nun who could barely read and could not write but prayed every moment for those in need and who at the moment of death assured us that she was committed to the salvation of all: "Take heart; I will pray for you."

And yet, beyond these outward appearances, Escrivá and Bakhita share more than one point of contact. Their spiritualities, however much rooted in enormously different cultural backgrounds, were in perfect harmony. One of the constant teachings of Josemaría Escrivá, writes Claudio Sorgi in his biography *Il padre* [The father], "was that of fulfilling one's ordinary tasks in an extraordinary manner", in the awareness that "when souls accept" God's plan for them, "even if they do not know where it will lead them and what it means, great masterpieces issue forth as a result." It is difficult not to envision Bakhita within this luminous Christian perspective.

But not only this. Josemaría Escrivá's most famous work, *The Way*, begins with these words: "Don't let your life be sterile. Be useful. Blaze a trail. Shine forth with the light of your faith and of your love. With your apostolic life wipe out the slimy and filthy mark left by the impure sowers of hatred. And light up all the ways of the earth with the fire of Christ that you carry in your heart." In another context, the Opus Dei founder wrote:

> During Holy Mass, I pray not only for my children, for my parents, for my brothers and sisters, for the parents and brothers and sisters of my children, but also for those who want

to injure us and those who have maligned us ... I say, "Lord, I forgive them in order that you might forgive them and in order that you might forgive our sins. I offer this Mass for their souls, just as I offer it for my children, for my parents, and for the parents of my children. The same for all." In this way, the Lord is pleased, and I feel satisfied ... We need to know how to forgive. Then if someone tells you that this is heroic, you can start laughing. It is a very beautiful thing. Does God not forgive us when we offend him? How can we, then, not forgive others?

For both Bakhita and Escrivá, therefore, forgiveness was the natural starting point for living the new life Christ offers, and it is a powerful sign of salvation held out to all men. Forgiveness and prayer.

Prayer is a charism that Bakhita shared with Magdalene of Canossa (1774–1835). Reading the Rule written by the foundress, however challenging a task it was for Mother Josephine, was always one of her daily points for meditation. For Bakhita, Magdalene was an example to follow. It was not by chance that in her final days, when more and more frequently she made references to heaven both to herself and to the sisters who tended to her, she described Magdalene as being present there, next to our Lady, waiting to welcome her home.

Magdalene is an example of charity, of joy in life, and of holiness. A "woman devoured by the fever of love" is the way Pope John Paul II described her in his homily during her canonization on September 2, 1988. A woman whose life was an exhortation to place oneself in a constant relationship with God. For Magdalene, prayer is the most precious time in one's life, an appointment with your God, with your All. "One is to embrace and value prayer more than study," Magdalene wrote to the Sons of Charity, her congregation's male branch, "the efficacy of prayer more than our own efforts, the power of prayer above all eloquence, and the science of prayer above every other form of knowledge."

These are words that Bakhita applied literally in her own life and that bore the maximum fruits of charity. In spite of the huge cultural and social differences that existed between the two saints (one descending from ancient nobility, the other an ex-slave), Magdalene and Bakhita both viewed prayer as a potent vehicle of God's love for the salvation of mankind. In her *Memoirs*, Magdalene writes: "I offer myself to be divided up into so many atoms of dust just to see the Lord glorified, and even to suffer hell in order that nobody should have to go there." This is a concept that Bakhita in her simplicity expressed in one of the many sayings of hers that have come to us through the testimony of those who heard them: "O Lord, I wish I could fly to my people and preach to them in a loud voice about your goodness. May everyone come to know and love you." Magdalene, after all, believed that "Jesus Christ is not loved because he is not known."

Magdalene and Bakhita both spent hours praying and meditating before the crucifix and before the Eucharist. These were moments of contemplation and also of utter surrender before Christ—experiences that are profoundly different from each other but that are shared by the great mystics. Saint Teresa of Ávila explains: "Prayer does not consist in thinking much, but in loving much." She taught that it is not necessary to say many things but, rather, to place oneself lovingly at the feet of Jesus. To that Thérèse of the Child Jesus adds: "Jesus does not ask great deeds from us, but only abandonment and gratitude."

We have many accounts of conversations people had with Bakhita about death. One day, for example, Sister Martini recalled that Bakhita, with her humble spirituality, became concerned that she did not know the proper words of greeting to use upon arrival in paradise. Her superior suggested that she greet the Lord and our Lady at the same time. But Bakhita considered that the traditional Canossian greeting, "May Jesus and Mary be praised", would leave out the other two Persons of the Trinity. Then, when it was suggested that she use the Glory Be as her greeting, she became cheerful once again.

Bakhita spoke so much about heaven in her final months that one priest, with tongue in cheek, asked her on one occasion how she could be so sure God would welcome her into the glory of the saints. Not concerned in the least, she replied that her *Paròn* would decide, and "he will put me where he wants me to be. When I am with him and where he wants me to be, then all will be well."

In the days preceding her death, another anecdote came to light that is full of spiritual and theological significance. As we know, Bakhita often gained inspiration from experiences in everyday life. In this case, she recalled the time during the war when she worked in the field hospital and every captain had an attendant who followed behind him carrying two suitcases, his own and one belonging to the officer.

At least three sisters who cared for Bakhita during her last days told the same anecdote. Mother Martini, Mother Dalla Costa, and Mother Clementina Calza recalled how Bakhita addressed each one of them personally, even though she repeated the same story over again. The following testimony from Sister Calza, who lived in Schio from 1919 to 1947, was offered during the beatification process:

One evening I went to visit her when she was very sick, and I asked her how she was. She replied, "I am worn out because I have two suitcases to carry, and both are heavy." I thought she might be delirious, but then she explained what she meant: "The officers have an attendant. And so the captain is Jesus, I am his attendant, and I carry two suitcases. One is mine, full of debts, the other is full of the merits of Jesus. As soon as I am at heaven's gate, I will cover my debts with the merits of our Lady, and then I will open the other suitcase and say: 'Eternal Father, now judge according to what you see.'" Then some other sisters came in, and she repeated the same thing to them with a few variations.[3]

Commenting on the unique analogy of the two suitcases in his book *Ritratti di santi* (Portrait of saints), Father Antonio Maria Sicari explains: "She wanted to arrive before the Father Almighty carrying her suitcase and the suitcase of her captain, Jesus. The *Paròn* would have had her open up the two suitcases. He would see the many sins in her own suitcase and then would see in the heavier one (it is described this way in Sister Martini's account) all the many merits of Jesus. She would then be welcomed with joy, for she had carried this suitcase as well. As you can see, the most arduous pages of theology, those dealing with justification, can be explained perfectly well by an old, illiterate nun."

As Sister Antonietta Filippin recalled, Bakhita was a woman who placed infinite trust in God and who had made of her life a continuous act of thanksgiving, of gratitude: "She always

[3] The teacher Ada Maraschin, who went to the Canossians' teaching high school in Schio beginning in 1938 and later taught there during the 1946–1947 academic year, reported a much shorter and more immediate version: "The important thing is to come to Jesus at the end of your life with two suitcases: a heavy one full of merits, and a light one with sins and defects."

looked death in the face with a cheerful soul. At the very end she also said that death carries us to God. And to those of us who said rather that God's judgment was frightening, she replied, "Do now what you would wish to do at that moment: judgment is what we do now."

At the beginning of 1946, with the illness showing no signs of relenting, Bakhita told one of the sisters that she would not make it through the end of the year. When December came and went, the same sister approached Bakhita and jokingly reminded her about her prediction. With her ever-present smile, Bakhita replied, "I had counted the days my way, and the Lord had counted them his way."

One day in 1922, during the very serious pneumonia that brought Bakhita close to death, the doctor who was caring for her came for a visit. Entering her room and finding her in good spirits, with a gentlemanly flourish he quoted to her a line from the Song of Songs (1:5): "Nigra sum sed formosa" (I am black but beautiful). Mother Josephine caught the reference immediately and responded with delight: "Oh, how I hope to hear those words when the Lord greets me."

One of Bakhita's constant thoughts, therefore, concerned her ultimate union with her *Paròn*. Constant and also very beautiful—one could even say "transfiguring". In the final days, a nun who had been visiting with her in her room, upon getting ready to leave and thinking these words would console her in the midst of her suffering, remarked: "Mother Josephine, I leave you now on your Calvary." Bakhita replied: "Not on Calvary—I am on Tabor." The nun, perhaps imagining that Bakhita had not understood the scriptural reference, explained: "We will go to Tabor after; now in our suffering we are on Calvary." Her reply was the same: "No, no, I am on Tabor."

These were days when Mother Bakhita pondered with ever greater frequency the moment of her eternal reward. And her conversation about death and paradise remained serene, level-headed, and joyful. Bakhita had discovered the secret of sanctity, and she lived it to the full right to the end.

Father Giuseppe Dossetti, in what many consider to be his spiritual testament, writes: "The way we approach joy is, paradoxically, precisely the way we approach death—one act at a time, in order that each moment might be lived ever more deeply as an act of faith. . . . It is a paradox, but a Christian paradox . . . How are we to approach death? By beginning to live serenely in its shadow with faith, letting our faith permeate our very existence. Because when death comes it will be difficult. . . . For this reason we must strive to understand that the supreme act of our death is truly the supreme act of our joy, even if out of natural instinct we rebel against all of this. . . . Then our joy will be great, even if nature rebels."

These words find perfect fulfillment in Bakhita's witness. For in every circumstance she lived out of the joyful encounter with the *Paròn*, trusting that she would be given the grace to walk the way of faith.

"Mother Josephine, do you not feel the pain, the adversity?" she was asked by those who were amazed by her extraordinary capacity for acceptance and surrender. Her response is a great lesson on the meaning of life: "Yes, I feel it. But when nature wants something, I say: 'Be good, little body of mine, you are always being treated like a queen. Be content with what you have. Tonight, tomorrow, we will see. . . .' And I go forward like this, and little by little the suffering, the desire calms down. I think about the sufferings of Jesus and his Mother and I do not listen to nature any further."

told me: 'Do you think it is easy to please the *Paròn*? But I do all that I can. He does the rest.' "

A life of prayer

Bakhita's life was one of unceasing prayer. Every moment of the day, every instant could be lived "together with the *Paròn*". Many remember how she always carried a prayer book with her or one on doctrine (the Catechism of Pius X) or the Canossian Rule. Often she would stop in the church and pray for hours, "as still as a statue" or "prostrate on the floor". At other times during the day she prayed the rosary continuously.

Bakhita had a great devotion to our Lady, which was born, as we have seen, at the Institute of Catechumens in Venice. "She loved me before I even knew who she was", she often affirmed. During the month of May, she taught the children of the guest lodgers in the Schio house to make little sacrifices in honor of the Virgin: "Sometimes", Sister Dalla Costa recounts, "when asked how many rosaries she had prayed that day, she would reply, 'I do not know; the *Paròn* keeps track of them, and our Lady helps to count as well, because it is her rosary.' "

"She had a special devotion to the Immaculate Heart of Mary", Sister Antonietta Filippin made a point of recalling. "Even though the Canossians cultivated devotion to Our Lady of Sorrows. When she was near death, she told me, 'I am fortunate, and the Lord loves me, for I entered the congregation on the feast of the Immaculate Conception, and it is only a few days now until the feast of our Lady's apparition at Lourdes." [4]

[4] February 11.

And Sister Martini added: "She recited the rosary constantly. I often asked her for whom she offered it, and sometimes she would say: 'To have holy patience.' When she was much older and was unable to meditate with her prayer book, she told me that she meditated on the life of Jesus so as to learn how to be more loving."

Sister Dalla Costa continued, unable to conceal her admiration:

> During Holy Week, I saw her weeping many times as she contemplated our Lord's Passion before a large crucifix in the choir, behind the altar . . . During free moments and without drawing attention to herself, she would go to the church to adore the Eucharist. She attended Mass with great reverence and attentiveness. She much preferred priests who did not rush through the celebration of Mass. She received Communion every day, and when she was in good health, she regularly approached the sacrament of penance. She did not perform practices out of habit, but with genuine fervor and a spirit of recollection. I observed her with both curiosity and edification, hoping to benefit from her example. She was devoted to the pious exercise of the Stations of the Cross, and she offered it for the souls in purgatory; she repeated it each day, even at times when it was not prescribed. Her spirit was moved as she stood before each station. I always saw her absorbed in prayer. She prayed to her guardian angel that he might help her remember her duties. She recited the Angel of God prayer twelve times as Magdalene of Canossa did.

Turning to the testimony of Sister Filippin, we read that Bakhita "cultivated a particular devotion for the Holy Eucharist, with which she was in love. The Eucharist was at the center of her faith. She was very happy as a sacristan, for this office allowed her to be closer to the tabernacle."

She continued:

> Bakhita continually prayed for the propagation of the faith, she who knew firsthand what it means not to have faith. She prayed to the Lord and was convinced that he would grant her request that the members of her family might come to know the faith ... She had unlimited hope in the Lord. She lived from God. Even if she was provided with mediocre texts for meditation, she had very profound thoughts that enabled her to understand her deep union with God. She was moved to tears thinking about the graces and the goodness God bestowed upon her, for being called to baptism and to the religious life. She prayed and offered sacrifices for the conversion of pagans and sinners and for the missions.

Sister Noemi Raccanello, who lived in close contact with Bakhita beginning in 1919, recalled how the African nun's life reflected her desire for God:

> I think that Mother Bakhita's deep prayer life was the fruit of her living, humble, and active faith, which pervaded her prayer. Her spirit of faith was the very life of her life. In practice, she saw beyond persons, things, events; she did not remain fixed on immediate causes but ascended right away to the prime mover, God, whether the causes were small and insignificant or exceptional. She was always ready to interrupt her work when she was called, no matter who called her. Always willing to consent to any request made of her, to go down to the parlor or the courtyard to meet whoever wanted to see her. Always obliging to answer the questions of those who were curious.

So mature was her faith, tested and refined through prayer and suffering, that on occasion it seemed worlds apart from what are considered normal and prudent ways of thinking, so much so that she might come across as naïve or as something of a simpleton. Sister Raccanello continued:

> During the last war [WWII] she was transported to a room that was less exposed and dangerous (or at least so we thought), together with another nun who had remained for seven hours under the debris of the Canossian house in Vicenza that had been bombarded. Mother Bakhita, already unable to move without assistance from others, did her best to soothe and reassure her that the planes overhead were making noise but would soon go away without causing any casualties. And she spoke with such simplicity and confidence that she succeeded in calming her companion completely. On other occasions, she would repeat: "The planes drop bombs, but God is in control of them. We are in his hands, and we are mistaken if we tremble and are afraid. Let us be good and pray and have confidence in the Lord."

Theology of humility, theology of forgiveness

"The saints are messengers of God. It is God who sends them on a mission according to our needs and his plans." These words were written in reference to Bakhita by Canossian Father Amedeo Cencini, professor of pastoral theology at the Pontifical Salesian University in Rome and a consultor for the Congregation for Institutes of Consecrated Life and Societies of Apostolic Life. Looking at Bakhita and all the people who come to Christ through her, it is practically impossible even to imagine the shape of God's plan in the face of such immense needs as the persecution of Sudan, rich countries less and less inclined to charity, thousands of people from countries in the southern hemisphere who emigrate, as did Bakhita, to the north each day, the difficult relationship between religions, above all between Christians and Muslims, and the lack of love that wounds the hearts of millions of children every day.

Why did God send Bakhita to us? According to Father Divo Barsotti, theologian and founder of the Community of the Children of God,

> Bakhita is proof that Christianity can transform slaves, that is, people who have lost the sense of their own personhood, into persons capable of unexpected strength. Bakhita is the certainty that through Christ man can pass from a state of marginalization to one of eternal dignity, greatness, and freedom. And this applies not only to Africa, of course, but to the whole world. Christianity's powerful promotion of human dignity through figures such as Bakhita is enormous, even though it is often barely reported. A fundamental component of this movement is the promotion of the dignity of women, in opposition to the way in which women are reduced to objects, fashioned into slaves either by consumerism or by cultures that ignore their tremendous human, spiritual, and social gifts. Nobody has done more for women than Christianity, and Bakhita is a witness to this truth.

Bakhita is thus a sign of the liberation of the human person. But she is also a sign of the redemptive power of forgiveness. As Father Cencini emphasized,

> While the entire Church follows the path of conversion and reconciliation, while John Paul II, calls for and offers forgiveness, inviting everyone to purify his memory, a model is proposed to us—a Sudanese woman. In Bakhita there is something particularly original, something that helps us to understand the most profound meaning of reconciliation,

especially the most difficult kind: reconciliation with our past and our past wounds. It is not enough to forgive or ask for forgiveness, to overlook transgressions or pretend nothing ever happened. Much less can we forget wrongs and injustices. The purification of memory is a slow and complex process of reading one's past through faith. It involves a total reexamination of one's own history, especially those areas that are hardest and most difficult to accept. Our memory is purified when we are actively able to give a new meaning even to what is negative, to evil inflicted and received—to sin—transfiguring it so that it may be accepted and lived in a positive way, no longer with bitterness or resentment toward others or oneself. From her own experience of slavery and of violent and perverse encounters, Bakhita could have emerged with a disintegrated personality, with a heart full of resentment and despair, with the temptation to repress or ignore wounds that were still raw, still open. Instead, the encounter with the Christian faith became an experience that allowed her to gather together her entire past without fighting any of its ghosts, without throwing it away and forcing herself to forget about it, without the satisfaction of being able to forgive those who had done her wrong. Bakhita does much, much more with the help of grace: she succeeds in fully integrating the evil that was done to her. She gives it a new meaning, transforms and transfigures it, and goes so far as to live it as a blessing. "If I were to meet those slave traders who kidnapped me and those who tortured me," she affirms, "I would get down on my knees and kiss their hands, because if that had not happened, I would not be a Christian or religious today."

According to Father Cencini, then, in Bakhita, in her encounter with God, we see a typically biblical situation take flesh in history once again, what I call the "theology of nothingness", that is, the special attention God pays to the nothingness of man. There are many biblical episodes where God is irresistibly attracted to situations in which man finds himself overwhelmed by loss, weakness, humiliation. We could think of the widow during the time of Elijah, the widow in Elisha's time, the multiplication of loaves, the Good Samaritan, Mary Magdalene . . . When man, like Elijah's widow, "embraces his nothingness" and recognizes his existential reality, he attracts God's sympathy. And God's blessing descends upon him. Thus it is with Bakhita . . . No one ever could have imagined that this little slave would have a glorious future, yet today her "nothingness" is an expression of God's eternal All.

VI

Woman of Great Humanity

Living witnesses

Many of the testimonies and episodes presented in this book are drawn from both the ordinary beatification proceedings and from the apostolic proceedings in Vicenza. However, there are many people still alive today who knew Bakhita and who can share recollections about her as well as conversations they had with her. These come mainly from women who live in Schio or in the region of Veneto who as children either spent time in the orphanage or attended kindergarten or one of the other schools on Via Fusinato. There are also some priests, like Father Giovanni Munari, who as a child served as an altar boy for the sisters when Bakhita was sacristan—a man who owes almost everything to Bakhita, even his life. Then there those who, like Father Gabriele Amorth (whose testimony we presented earlier), saw the Sudanese nun during her travels promoting the foreign missions. There are a number of Canossian nuns as well, and there are other people who today still consider themselves Bakhita's relatives, namely, the direct descendants of Illuminato Checchini. Finally, there are women who bear Bakhita's very name, as a sign of devotion and esteem that in some African regions is becoming a tradition, one that might soon spread to Italy.

In speaking with these living witnesses, an image of Bakhita emerges that is profoundly human, joyful, even funny. It shows a woman always thoughtful and attentive to the needs of whomever she was with at that moment. These are qualities that often did not shine through in the official documents—aimed, after all, at investigating her sanctity and life of virtue—or that in one way or another were toned down.

Bakhita was a cheerful woman. Above all she was serene and at peace with herself. As a result, she was able to inspire confidence and tranquility in whoever would stop for a moment to speak with her or who might have had occasion to observe how intent she was to fulfill her simple daily tasks. She was so good and willing to be of service that people often thought she was naïve. In any case, she was incapable of generating misunderstandings or hard feelings around her, not even inside the large religious communities in which she lived. Children, ever sensitive to the human qualities of people they meet, loved her so much that they went looking for her, then asked to see her again as soon as they could.

Maria Borghesan is a youthful eighty-five-year-old who lives in Schio. She knew Bakhita when she attended the Canossians' school for girls at the age of nine. Then the young Maria returned to live with her parents at home. But when she and her family subsequently had a falling out, the young girl found in Bakhita the support that allowed her, as she herself admits, to survive.

After the separation, I went to Bakhita. She was like a mother. "Be patient, Maria. I understand how you feel, because I too have had many hurts." She spoke to me like that after giving me a kiss and taking me under her arm. She told me: "Bear with it and you will see." I do not know if I could have kept on going without Bakhita. When I met her, she would become all beautiful, though she was all black. You just had to see her.

I never saw her lonely or sad. She was always surrounded by children. She was never alone. She always gave you a sweet or a piece of bread from her pocket. And she was very sensitive and able to understand people's problems. She became a little embarrassed when we children asked her if we could see the tattoos on her arm.

A short time before she died, she made it known that she would like to see me. Entering the room, I asked, "How are you, Mother?" She replied, "Fine, I am here with my *Parón*." She always had the *Parón* on her mind. That day we spoke a long time. Then, before I left, she said, "Always stay the way you are. Remember, I will always be here for you." To this day I still ask her for help, and I seem to see her just as she was when she was smiling at us children. She had a word for everyone, with her extraordinary sensitivity. She had a natural way of speaking, an upright posture, and she always smelled like perfume. I still keep one of her handkerchiefs.

Santa Faccin, now eighty years old, went to the Canossians' kindergarten in Schio.

"My parents dropped me off at the portress' booth, and the Little Brown Mother would take care of me. At times she would take all of us to church. When she sat next to me, she would gently stroke my arm. Then she would tell us a story about her life."

Antonia, the youngest in the Munari family, also went to kindergarten in Schio. She attended in the second half of the 1930s, when Bakhita returned to the village in the Veneto region, having completed her tour for the missions. Antonia is the main character in one of the most delightful anecdotes in the saint's life—the one about chocolate.

"When I saw her for the first time I was four or five years old. I was with my oldest brother [Father Giovanni Munari]. Seeing her all black, I thought she was made of chocolate. So I licked her hand."

Antonia also recalled, "We children loved her a whole lot and every Sunday we made her tell us a story. She was a woman of great simplicity. Always available and patient toward everyone. I remember she was always ready with a one-liner. 'Sister, how come you still have so many teeth left?' I asked her one day with the other children. She replied quickly, smiling: 'Because I do not eat so many sweets like you.'"

Maria Pia Checchini is among those who retain vivid memories of Bakhita. She lives in Padua, and, as we have already seen, she is the great granddaughter of Illuminato and great grandniece of Pius X: "Bakhita was like family to us: an aunt, really. Whenever she was passing through Padua, she would come and visit us. I was a child, but I remember her well. She brought us candies and some little gifts."

She speaks about these gifts with a soft smile on her lips. A serene smile, tinged with both shyness and protectiveness as she takes from her purse the two small, hand-sewn objects that Bakhita made for her out of glass beads. These are similar to the other items we have described already, such as the holy card of the angel leading a child to the altar, given to Maria Pia for her first Communion, with a hand-written message and signature: Bakhita.

Even today we can find Bakhita's signature inscribed across the globe in fresh ink. It belongs to women, girls, and babies who have received the gift of Bakhita's name, even in Italy (in Africa—above all in Sudan, Congo, and Uganda—this name is becoming commonplace among Christians; in recent years the name has spread through Latin America). It is an authentic sign that Bakhita's holiness is destined to make inroads—past the distractions and egoism and into the heart of contemporary Western society—because it is not a traditional name. In Italy, Bakhita is used mainly as a middle name. There are some, however, who bear Bakhita as a first name.

Bakhita Sartor is one of these "lucky" women, and she herself underscores this point. She was born in Padua in 1969, the year Mother Josephine's body was exhumed and moved from the public cemetery to the Canossian cemetery on Via Fusinato. For this occasion, the weekly newspaper *Christian Family* published a substantial profile of the Sudanese ex-slave, at the time a Servant of God, whom everybody considered a saint and who had been the source of many miracles and answered prayers. The Sartor husband and wife read the article and were so affected by it that they decided to name their daughter Bakhita.

As little Bakhita grew up, she began to ask why she had been given such a strange name. Her parents explained the circumstances, but she wanted to know more. As soon as she was old enough, she embarked on a journey through Italy, traveling in the footsteps of the saint. She read the books that recount her story, and she went to Schio. Here she visited the Sudanese nun's tomb and spoke at length with a nun who had known Mother Bakhita. Slowly but surely, the name the girl had once found somewhat uncomfortable acquired rich layers of ever deeper meaning, and even for those who lived around her the name became normal and pleasing. Bakhita Sartor is very proud of it, and she knows that she is truly "Lucky". She says:

> The example of Josephine Bakhita is more relevant than ever. She never carried out very important tasks but always

did humble jobs, and she was not educated. These are all things that are in sharp contrast with today's vision of life. Yet she was completely fulfilled and has become a saint. And there are innumerable things to learn from her, from which today's world would benefit were they put into practice. For example, the ability to find value in the evil one suffers rather than cultivating hate or ending in despair. Her humility is a wonderful example. And there is also something I admire tremendously: the way in which she accepted the Word with joy—how she immediately felt liberated and saved by the good news.

Stories of priests and of Father Giovanni Munari—the man for whom Bakhita offered her life

Father Giovanni Munari[1] is a spry octogenarian who serves as parish priest in the hamlet of Fongara, in the province of Vicenza. His recollections of Bakhita are so numerous that without exaggeration one could say they span a lifetime— his own. It is a life marked indelibly by Mother Josephine's constant presence and her prayers of intercession on his behalf.

He first came to know Bakhita when he was approximately two years old. Born in 1920, he and his father, mother, grandmother, and four siblings lived next door to the Canossian convent in Schio. His family was on very friendly terms with the sisters, and little Giovanni was in frequent contact with them. He served as an altar boy for

[1] Father Munari is also the author of the first guidebook for lodging accomodations offered by convents and religious orders in Italy, Europe, and around the world. Often plagiarized and copied by others, it is entitled *Itinerantibus*. It can be found in specialized bookstores and is published in regularly updated editions.

the sisters in the summer of 1927 and then nearly without interruption from 1929 to 1935. He recalled, "There was often another boy with me, who later became a Franciscan... Every now and then, when Mother Josephine was sacristan and I did not arrive on time for Mass, she would come get me." He also encountered her every morning at her portress' station at the front door of the convent, for he accompanied his youngest sister, Antonia, to and from nursery school each day.

When he received his vocation, Giovanni left for the seminary in Vicenza. These were the years when Bakhita was traveling to promote the missions. Giovanni inspired other seminarians to read *Tale of Wonder*, and then with the permission of his superiors he organized a meeting with Mother Josephine. She told the seminarians her life story, and afterward she made a point of reiterating, "Remember to be holy priests." Praying for priests was a staple of the African nun's intercessory intentions. She prayed for the Pope and above all for missionaries. With regard to priests, Sister Anna Dalla Costa remembered that Bakhita used to say, "When a priest speaks it is God who is speaking, it is God who inspires him. The priest is an instrument in God's hands."

"During my seminary years," continued Father Giovanni, "another priest who knew Bakhita as a young man, Monsignor Zaffonato, archpriest of Valdagno, later bishop of Udine, used to take his catechism students each year on a pilgrimage to visit Bakhita. They would leave on foot in the morning with a sack lunch and then return in the evening."

Gathering together a few more memories that sprang to mind, Father Giovanni added: "Then there is my seminary classmate who is a Comboni missionary in Africa. His name is Father Francesco Grotto. Chased out of Sudan, he went to Togo. There he built several small churches. One of them is constructed in the shape of an African bread oven. It is dedicated to the Eucharist because Bakhita was a sacristan. In 1995 a statue of Bakhita was brought there, and now they want to dedicate that church to Saint Bakhita."

In 1941, while he was a seminarian, Father Giovanni fell ill with tuberculosis, and in 1942 one of his lungs collapsed. His health plummeted, and the doctors feared for his life. His mother rushed to Bakhita, asking for her prayers. This was during the height of the war, and we know how the African nun by now had a reputation for holiness among the people. Bakhita listened to the woman whom she had known for thirty years. She replied with a smile, "Do not worry. Giovanni will become a priest. I am offering my life for him."

Giovanni recovered, became a priest, and then a pastor throughout the Veneto region. His mother never told him about the grace received through Bakhita's intercession (and Father Giovanni made no mention of this incident during his testimony for the diocesan beatification proceedings). Father Giovanni finally heard about it in 1983, when this episode was already considered by many proof of the saint's love for the Church and her ministers. With this new knowledge, Father Giovanni was able to look back on his life and interpret a number of events in light of this grace that he had received.

For example, in 1954, "my brother, when he went for his military medical exam in Verona, asked me to go with him because if he could prove that I had contracted TB, they would exempt him from service. My brother, however, had to fulfill his military service after all, because after a complete medical examination, following the story I told them about my illness, they could find no trace of tuberculosis. I had been healed so well that it was as if I never had TB."

A decade earlier, in 1944, during the partisan war, Father Giovanni was serving as pastor of Saint Boniface Church, near Verona.

In November, when the Allied air raids were particularly intense, I was urgently needed in Verona. I jumped on my bicycle and about a half a mile from the city I realized that a plane was bombing the train station and strafing it with machine-gun fire. I stopped and waited for the raid to end. When I started out again, right when I got back on the road, I was immediately run over by a German car racing out of the city. But nothing happened to me at all.

On my way back to Saint Boniface's, I realized that the bridge at Montebello had been blown up. There was no other way across but to wade. While I was in the middle of the river with water up to my waist, what should appear out of the blue but a "Pippo" (the nickname for the reconnaissance planes that also served to harass the population), and it began machine-gunning me. Bullets rained down all around me, zinging through water, but I ended up walking away without so much as a scratch.

Stories like these are enough to give one chills, but even more so when they are linked to Bakhita's promise: "I am offering my life for him." Father Giovanni told the stories calmly, with a smile on his face, in the same manner as he recounted the rest of his religious life, which came to fruition under the protection of a friend and saint. In all the stories from people whose lives have been touched in a special way by Bakhita, a constant feature stands out: an instinctive lack of sensational language, as if these things were everyday events.

In the same tone, Father Giovanni told the story of his last encounter with the African nun, three days before she died. However, in this instance, his matter-of-fact tone little by little lost its customary detachment.

It was the fifth of February, 1947. In those days I often went to the Canossian school in Schio to say Mass. After the celebration, I brought Communion to Bakhita in her room. When I entered she told me, "Yesterday Father Alessandro came to give me extreme unction, but he did not commend my soul to God. Could you do that for me?" So I began to recite the prayer of commendation in Italian. At every verse she let out an exclamation that revealed her transparent desire to reach her celestial destination as soon as possible.

"Go forth, O Christian soul, from this world," the prayer said, and in response, with an ecstatic gaze, Bakhita replied, "I want to go, I want to go!"

"In the name of God the Father who created you,
in the name of Jesus Christ the Son who has
    redeemed you,
in the name of the Holy Spirit who has
    sanctified you . . .
May the angels come to welcome you . . ."

And at every pause, she repeated joyously: "Yes, yes!"

"My encounter with Bakhita"

This is the title given to the four typewritten pages signed by Teresa Cortese Grandotto, a teacher, dated January 27, 2000. They report her extraordinary meeting with the African nun. We have preserved this title just as we have preserved the text that follows, with only a few abridgments for reasons of space.

I was twelve years old when I made my first trip without my parents. I had to go with some of my classmates, six or seven, from Asiago to Schio to take the middle school entrance exam for homeschoolers. Middle schools in the plateau regions did not yet exist. I was very excited about the exam and the trip ... If it did not go well, I would have surely had to learn a trade or to remain at home to help my mother.

It was decided that we would stay three days at the Canossian school ... The time came for my departure on the rack railway train. Our teacher accompanied us, placed us under the care of the mother superior, and wished us all good luck. We all loved being at the school. We explored up and down the hallways, and we met many other girls ...

But our biggest surprise came that evening, right before going to bed. At the end of a long dark corridor on the top floor, we saw a figure approach, holding a small lamp. We stopped, a little bit afraid, because we did not know who it was, and we could not see the person's face. At a certain point, I was able to make out white teeth and eyeballs. The rest was completely dark.

The figure had halted as well, a few steps away from us, smiling, and raised the lamp up to our faces and to hers. Only then did we realize that in front of us stood an African nun. This was the first person of color I had ever seen. We were all silent and unable to move. Then she began to speak.

"Where are you from? Are you afraid of me? What is your name?" she asked me. I answered and explained that the next day we had to take an entrance exam. Then, looking at her, I said, "I am very afraid!"

She smiled, stroked my head, then motioned for me to kiss the medal around her neck, saying, "I will pray for you and your classmates, but the *Paròn* will take care of it for you." She rested her hand on my head again, and then I grew calm.

I have never forgotten that smile and that touch. She could easily have walked straight ahead and avoided us; but she did not. She wanted to stop and give us a kind word, even though her words were hard to understand and even though her black skin, in that era, could have made her and us feel somewhat awkward.

I went to sleep in peace and thought about what that extraordinary person had told me. I knew that they called her the Little Brown Mother and that her name was Bakhita. I felt I had just had an important encounter. The exam went very well for two of us, and I returned home happy . . .

One time I felt a strong and sudden desire to do a watercolor painting of Bakhita as a child in chains. I gave it as a gift to a dear friend, and a short time ago I saw it again in her room above her nightstand.

During the time when nobody imagined she would be beatified, I spoke about her to my students at school and in catechism class. They were struck and fascinated by the story of her life. I continued spreading her story later through books and videocassettes . . .

I can still feel her touch and her voice. Often I ask her about things, and, just as she did in the past, Bakhita reassures me and smiles at me. On several occasions she has taken me by the hand and opened doors.

In January 1992, the canonical recognition of the mortal remains of Bakhita took place at the Canossians' church in Schio. Our bishop was even there, and you could only enter if you were invited. I did not have an invitation, but I approached the church in order to pray . . . It was then that Bakhita took me by the hand and showed me inside . . .

A man from Caritas had arrived with some Africans, and he asked me if I could be their host and take them into the church, find them a place to sit, and keep them company. Without even looking for it, I found myself in this situation and ended up sitting in one of the very front pews . . .

I was very moved, and I felt her very close to me. It seemed as though she were speaking to me in her husky voice: "Now, what are you going to do? The *Paròn* has decided to do it this way, without an invitation!"...

After the Mass, I got ready to return home. A special room had been prepared where the recognition of Bakhita's mortal remains was taking place. I was able to see a little inside the room as I passed by the corridor, but I knew that I could not enter. But just then a sister approached me, inviting me in. She specifically called me aside ... Everything that day was mysterious and inexplicable to me. I entered the room and nobody told me to stand in back or was surprised that I was there. That sister who was so kind and good stood by my side, explaining many things, and I understood through her that Bakhita had once again given me a gift.

Woman of the people, woman of wit

Sister Calza said, "I always saw that Bakhita was very obliging to people, humble, and she had a sense of humor, too. During community recreation, she was able to overcome her natural bashfulness and could tell stories for the amusement of the sisters. With her imperfect Italian, she unwittingly triggered much hilarity. Afterward she was willing to repeat whatever she had said that made us laugh, if she was invited to do so, and when sisters from other communities were visiting ours."

This way of behaving was a constant in Bakhita. She never shied away from sharing with others the joy that fueled her life. And she did so spontaneously—sometimes in order to enliven a community occasion and sometimes out of sheer delight in making people laugh through a funny gesture or word. Such delight is attributed by some to her friendship with Illuminato Checchini, a jovial man who loved cracking jokes, even when he was not playing the role of Massarioto.

Bakhita's light-hearted spirit and ready smile never seemed to wane, even during her last days. Among the many anecdotes from the saint's sickbed, we have one about a nun who visited Bakhita and was deeply affected by the sight of her emaciated condition. Out of sympathy, perhaps offering Bakhita something to eat, she exclaimed: "Mother Josephine, you are practically a skeleton now!" Cheerful as ever, Bakhita's immediate response was laughter, and then, feigning seriousness, she said, "When I die there will be a great deal of weeping." Struck both by the content and tone of this remark, the nun asked, "What do you mean?" Bakhita quickly replied, "The weeping of the worms . . . they will not find any meat on my bones and so they will all be weeping."

The list of anecdotes of this sort is very long. Some of them are particularly amusing.

At the apostolic beatification proceedings, Sister Angelina De Pretto recounted the story about the time when, as a young novice, she first visited the house at Schio. When she was introduced to Mother Bakhita, she took a step backward, astonished, and exclaimed: "How black she is!" Beaming her best smile, the African nun was prompt to reply: "But you know what? My soul is white!" One evening, a few days later, the same Sister Angelina crossed paths with Bakhita in a dimly lit corridor leading to the refectory. "Oh! Little Brown Mother!" she cried out, startled by her unexpected appearance. "Forgive me, but you are so black that I did not see you." Bakhita, serene as ever, responded, "And in the dark even you are no longer white." At that, they both start chuckling together.

From the official testimonies we also have the account about a person who had recently read the book *Tale of Wonder*, which cost two Italian lire at the time, and who had just arrived in Schio in order to see Mother Josephine. The community was gathered for recreation when the mother superior announced that this visitor had arrived and was waiting in the parlor. With her usual spontaneity, Bakhita responded with a quip that set off a chain reaction of laughter: "Mother, if it costs two lire to read about me, how much is it to see me?"

Then there is the story that has become one of the more famous ones in Schio and the Veneto region, even though it is transmitted only via oral tradition. Born in sub-Saharan Africa, Bakhita suffered in particular during the cold winter months in northern Italy, and everyone remembered how the portress' booth was a particularly chilly outpost. Thus, whenever someone came in or out and forgot to close the door, especially if he were a child, Bakhita would turn to him with a little glint in her eye and ask, "What was the name of Abraham's wife?" As soon as the name of Sarah came back in response, she would reply using the word *sara*, a play on the Venetan form of the verb "to close": "Then *sara* the door!"

Bakhita loved to laugh and make others laugh for the simple joy of laughing. Sister De Pretto remembered that every now and then, during community recreation, Bakhita would purposely recount certain little incidents that happened to her that would make the community laugh. For example, she would tell the story about the doctor who came to examine Bakhita's ailing leg, the one that had been kicked and gouged when she was a slave. After having the nun sit down on her bed, he asked her, "Now take off your sock." With deadpan humor, she replied, "Doctor, it is not possible, for the Lord has made me this way", alluding to the fact that she was not wearing a sock but had black skin.

Another quality that made people laugh was her occasional clumsiness, something that she herself liked to make fun of at times. For example, during recreation periods she would intentionally dance in a silly manner or would perform improbable gymnastic exercises or little theatrical skits. On one occasion Monsignor Longhin, the bishop of Treviso, made a visit to the Schio house. All the sisters were in the parlor. Bakhita was the first one he approached, and as she came forward to greet him and kiss his ring, she tripped and fell down at his feet. "Well done, Mother Josephine, you would like to show me what an oriental greeting looks like?" asked the bishop with a good-humored laugh. Swiftly Bakhita got back up, rearranged herself, and apologized with simplicity: "Forgive me for falling down in front of you!" The bishop replied straight away: "Forgive me for not picking you up!"

During the period of the field camp hospital, the captain's attendant who lived in a house in front of the convent one day rushed over to his window in order to see Bakhita passing through the courtyard below. He did not realize, however, that the windows were closed, and he smashed them with his head. Later he complained out loud to his fellow officers, "That black sister cost me five lire." Bakhita happened to be walking by and heard these remarks. With a laugh she responded, "He did not even call out to me. His curiosity would have cost him less if he had done so."

Bakhita was also able to translate into popular parlance, almost as if they were proverbs or sayings of Massarioto, great truths of the faith. These verbal expressions have surfaced in various sections of this biography already, such as the extremely powerful line about the Last Judgment: "Do now what you would wish to do at that moment: judgment is what we do now." Or her saying about total trust in divine providence: "I give everything to the *Paròn*, and he takes care of me—he is obliged to."

To one of the sisters who was anxious about her sufferings, Bakhita replied that she should ask the Lord for more, together with the capacity to bear them with patience, because "one needs to be cunning in this world and find ways of gaining as many merits as we can." Then she added, "With God in our heart, we can bear all things."

In the summer, she reminded the sisters who were complaining that it was too hot next to the big wood stove in the kitchen: "The place that is too hot is hell, and that is the only thing we need to be worried about."

Bakhita considered herself a great sinner, and when someone would comment that she led a virtuous life, she would answer: "What the *Paròn* sees is different from what others see." And again: "What appears beautiful is not beautiful but, rather, what is pleasing to the Lord."

To the women with families who came to ask her for advice, Bakhita always asked whether the husband loved the Lord, for she considered this to be the foundation for a successful marriage. If the women then confided their problems to her, Bakhita counseled that they "learn to be quiet and patient with their husbands in order to help them to become better."

The following expressions were clearly the fruit of her reflection on everyday life: "If in this life we do not hope in the Lord, what will we ever accomplish?" "People come and go, one after another. It is the will of God. But he always remains. In paradise, then, we will all see each other again: it is just a matter of waiting a little bit." We will close with the following utterly simple, almost naïve consideration, but one that brings us face to face with our own

conscience: "How fortunate you are to have been born in a Catholic country. I arrived here late. Be grateful to God and to our Lady."

Loved by children

We have already noted how Bakhita's outward attractiveness and her goodness had an immediate impact on the hearts of children, opening up space for a dialogue that more often than not would last well beyond childhood. Her knack for communicating with others, along with her attitude of availability, were among the special characteristics of this saint's charism. It was these qualities above all that helped her gain access to the hearts not only of children but of those who meet her today in the twenty-first century.

"One time", recalled Mother Raccanello, "I saw her in the courtyard surrounded by a group of young people who were so happy just to have her to themselves that they kept on asking her questions. One boy, perhaps a little indiscreetly, asked to see her tattoos. Bakhita, with modesty, pulled down a little her prayer shawl that she wore around her neck and allowed them all to see her scars. 'Poor little dears', she explained later to those who knew well how reserved she was. 'Why not satisfy their request? Who knows whether later on they might be more grateful to the Lord for having allowed them to be born in Italy.'"

Bakhita would tell the children stories about her life as a slave, leaving out certain details at times so as to spare them the cruel implications. The children were fascinated by these tales, and Bakhita took advantage of these occasions to recount episodes from the Old and New Testaments using the same storytelling technique. The story of Joseph—the young man sold by his brothers who would later become a powerful man in a foreign country—was Bakhita's favorite. It is a story that mirrors her own: she too was sold; she too landed on foreign soil and adapted to it; she too was ready to forgive those who had done evil to her.

Little children felt at ease with Mother Josephine. They felt free to be children—playing, speaking, being curious—even if they had already been touched by life's sadder realities. There is a beautiful story that dates back to 1908, told by Sister Giulia Campolongo, who was a missionary in India for several decades and who arrived at the Canossian house in Schio when she was seven years old. Unable to care for her by himself anymore, the father left her at the school in tears. A short time later, accompanied by a nun, she met Bakhita on the stairs:

> That black face filled me with fear at first. I felt like fleeing. Then I looked at her for a long time. Gazing back at me were two big, clear, eyes, full of goodness. Standing out against a black background were a beautiful line of smiling white teeth, while two gentle arms reached out to me. I looked back at her and then touched her, finally realizing that I was in the presence of a kind and good mother. From that moment on, I never shied away from the Little Brown Mother again. On the contrary, I always went looking for her, attracted by her simple, honest smile, which inspired such confidence.

Bakhita's buoyant spirit, her natural meekness, and her clumsiness were qualities the children found endearing. So much so that when they became aware (like the soldiers in the field hospital during WWII) that they could be on friendly terms with her, they then felt they could have a little fun at Mother Josephine's expense. One of these

humorous moments is described by Giovanna Santulin, who was ten at the time:

One day, I was coming out of church with all my class-mates in single file. We saw the Little Brown Mother car-rying a tray with breakfast for the priest. Suddenly she slipped and fell to the ground. I do not remember who had bumped her. The tray had flipped over and everything was smashed to pieces. Her bonnet even flew off her head. In a flash, however, she picked it up, but put it on backward. I cannot begin to tell you how much we laughed when we saw that. Yet what we found most edifying was that she did not lose her temper. With her usual, beautiful smile, she gathered up all the fragments and did not say a word.

And do not forget the affectionate relationship Bakhita maintained with little Mimmina, Mrs. Michieli's daughter, who clung to her legs and wept because her nanny did not want to go back to Africa with her. In her dictated mem-oirs, Mother Josephine related that it was difficult for her not to be deeply moved by the words of the little girl who loved her so much.

There was also another girl, during the time when Bakh-ita was a catechumen, who was struck by the Sudanese woman's availability and the manner in which she carried herself. Her name was Giulia Della Fonte. After Bakhita's death, she sent a letter from Milan, where she lived, to the nuns in Schio, addressed to Mother Genoveffa De Battisti, who was collecting material for the beatification. Her story began in the early months of 1889, when in Venice at the age of six she saw Bakhita for the first time, holding Mim-mina by the hand. These are childhood memories, to be read and judged accordingly.

I was just a child when Bakhita came to the Institute of the Catechumens. I saw her for the first time from the balcony of my house, which overlooked the linen room of the institute. The windows were open, and I had a vision of this black person who was holding a little girl by the hand ...

One day I was brought over to the institute, and I met her. I stroked her hand but did not know what to say to her because she was not familiar with the language. I got along well with the girl in her charge, and every day I was able to play with her. It was always the Little Brown one who looked after us. She was good, gentle, always smiling. But her smile seemed different from the others—to me it seemed a sad smile. She had tender feelings for her mistress, and the mistress' little daughter showed great affection for Bakhita. The girl wanted me to kiss her Bakhita, and I did so willingly, saying she was beautiful and good. One morning, coming downstairs as usual to the institute, I found only the Little Brown one, who greeted me in tears. My little friend had departed for Africa.

Then they told me that Bakhita would be baptized soon and that I too would attend ... At the ceremony I sat in the front row in the institute's little church ... I was very excited.

Afterward, with my mother and aunt, I was invited for refreshments in the parlor. Besides Cardinal Agostini, there were quite a few priests and many lords and ladies. I stood a little on the side and tried to get the Little Brown one's attention. I too wanted to get close to her and kiss her ... She saw me, smiled at me, and called me over, giving me a kiss. I was so happy and stayed right beside her. I remember there were sweets and drinks, but I did not taste anything. Nor did the Little Brown one, whom I now called Josephine.

When everybody had departed, the rector of the Institute of the Catechumens, Father Jacopo dei conti Avogadro, an old, holy man, invited her to lunch, and he invited

me too. We had lunch together, just the three of us, served by the priest's good housekeeper. The usual air of sadness on her face was now completely gone. She seemed transfigured. She spoke very little, but her happiness was shining through every gesture she made, every word she spoke.

I asked her what it felt inside during the ceremony, but she did not know what to say and only caressed me and smiled. I remember that I kissed her hands with the idea that she was a saint. At home I was told that baptism makes us saints, washes away our sins, and makes the soul whiter than white ... I then continued to see her often, always happy, always as if inspired.

VII

Universal Sister

Within the expression "universal sister" coined by Blessed John Paul II, we discover the pulsing heart of Bakhita's mission and message. Her holy witness speaks with extraordinary eloquence to our contemporary day and age: her spontaneous spirituality inspired by a love for simple things; her peace in the face of death and the great questions of life; her unconditional trust in God and the need to be always in contact with him; an exceptional goodness that expressed itself in the desire to forgive those who had enslaved and tortured her; and the absence of qualities that would lead one to mistreat others, such as presumption, intolerance, vengeance, the desire to affirm oneself, pride, the certainty of being right.

There is hardly a moment in Bakhita's life that could not benefit those seeking to make an honest reappraisal of their lives. And for those who happen upon the story of the illiterate black slave who became a saint in northern Italy, one of the areas most symbolic of European economic development in these last decades, it is hard not to experience a sense of admiration, if other emotions do not first prevail.

Her witness is as timely today as it was when you could meet her on the street, wearing her beat-up shoes and dressed in her clean yet threadbare habit, held together by her darning stitches. She was admired intensely, for example, by

Monsignor Giuseppe Mani, archbishop of the Military Ordinariate for Italy. He first learned about Bakhita in the early 1990s, when he was auxiliary bishop of the Eastern Sector of Rome. Today on the wall of his room hangs a picture of the saint, to whom he turns, he admits, "every day in my prayers, asking also for favors and intercessions".

Sister Dalla Costa, who lived with Bakhita for thirty-six years, states that "her faith was simply radiant ... She was an example to everyone, and everyone wanted to hear her and to speak with her ... A large cross-section of people took her spiritual counsel very much to heart." She had a gift for speaking directly and to the point, with simple words that communicated profound faith. "Her natural virtues", recalls Sister Eugenia Cherti, who attended school in Schio from 1923 to 1929, "consisted of her sweetness, calm, resignation, natural affection, and keen moral sensitivity ... She made us students really feel God's goodness. She would say, 'How good the *Paròn* is. How good he is. How could anyone not love the Lord.'"

There was nobody, as a result, who could have any ill will toward Bakhita. "During the school recess every morning," remembers Sister Ginevra Brunati, "she would come looking for me in haste. With her typical gentleness and speaking the Veneto dialect, she would say to me, 'Sister, come and have a little soup.'[1] I would reply that it was not necessary, I was young and strong, but she would insist, 'Go on, Sister, the road is long and you still have a lot to do! Go, do not worry about it, I will take care of the children.' You just could not refuse her. She spoke with such humility and thoughtfulness that it would have been an insult to say no."

[1] This took place in the early 1940s when Bakhita was more than seventy years old.

Humble and poor

"To the poor", recalls Sister Anna Dalla Costa, "she would have given the very clothes she was wearing. She showed great compassion for those who were hungry, and she would ask if they wanted even more than they asked for. Not too long ago, a woman who lives in Schio on Via Fusinato, Teresina Calesella, told me: 'When I was hungry and I told Mother Bakhita about it, I received not one but two ladles full of soup, and sometimes three." She often made it known that the rich should give to those in need. Somebody who was moved by her words to this effect made some substantial donations, which Bakhita brought to Mother Superior. She was very happy when the superior subsequently asked her to take the gift and distribute it to the poor."

Bakhita was able to express such sensitivity for those who suffer above all because of her own humility and interior poverty, a poverty of spirit stemming straight from the Beatitudes. "One time", says Sister Clementina Calza, "the superior reprimanded all of us about a fault for which nobody took responsibility. Mother Bakhita threw herself on her knees and apologized as if she were the one who had done it, while in reality she was not responsible. When something happened to her, she never justified herself but always said: 'I am such a poor simpleton. I do not know how to do anything! I do not know how to help the superior.' But she got along well with the Lord and spoke with him as a friend, with great trust, certain that she was understood. She was a great example to us."

"Giving her massages", recalls Sister Carlotta Fabruzzo, who also served as a nurse in the Schio house, "I was able to observe how racked with pain she was in her body. A deep wound in her right thigh really struck me, so much

The two suitcases, or: When we are no longer afraid of death

"After I die, I will not frighten anyone", Bakhita often remarked in the weeks preceding her death. She foresaw the crowds of men, women, and children who would flock to her to pay their final respects once she had passed away and perhaps even glimpsed the devotion she would be accorded throughout the world. But above all, it was Bakhita herself who did not fear death.

In this sense, we can perhaps view in a different light an incident that took place during the Great War, when Bakhita was working in the kitchen and military hospital. Some young soldiers assigned to kitchen duty decided to play a joke on her (maybe because she was black, maybe because she was a bit naïve and awkward, but certainly because she was amiable and open with them). These were boys, it turned out, who were afraid of death. In any case, "some of them", affirmed Sister Anna Dalla Costa, "wanted to see whether Mother Josephine was afraid of death. So they set off some kind of mechanical device that made a loud noise in Bakhita's hallway. She remained calm, as if nothing had happened. Surprised by this, the soldiers asked her, 'But aren't you afraid of dying?' She replied that she was indifferent about death and then made use of this occasion to speak to them more about it, concluding that 'whoever has his soul in order has no need to fear anything.'" These words clearly call to mind the words of Christ: "Why are you afraid? Have you no faith?" (Mk 4:40).

Bakhita, therefore, was not afraid of death. On the contrary, on more than one occasion she let it be known that she would prefer to die in order to be united with God. In this she very much resembled not only Saint Paul ("My desire is to depart and be with Christ, for that is far better"

[Phil 1:23]) but also Magdalene of Canossa. Magdalene's spiritual director had to urge her to stop desiring to die, for during certain periods of intense prayer and ecstatic rapture, she felt as though her soul had left her body. In this state, she wanted nothing else than to remain in complete closeness to God.[2]

The desire to die so as to be united with Christ and, at the same time, the awareness that above all else one must be obedient to one's God-given mission on earth—this double desire is something we find repeatedly in Bakhita, although expressed in more humble and spontaneous language. In this regard, it is interesting to note that none of the direct testimonies that have come down to us have suggested that Bakhita ever experienced any mystical or ecstatic phenomena or that she performed any extraordinary acts of penance.

As Sister Fabruzzo stated,

> In her final illness, she endured atrocious pain and suffering without complaint, and she preserved a cheerful, tranquil expression on her face. She said that the sufferings due to illness are more meritorious than any voluntary mortification. She thought about Christ's Passion and about Our Lady of Sorrows, and she said that we do not ever suffer as much as they do. For me it will always remain a mystery how Mother Josephine was able to be so serene, in control of her nerves, the same person day in and day out ... She

[2] Magdalene writes in her *Memoirs*: "I felt the power of God in a unique way draw my soul to be united with him ... I then experienced a great desire for heaven ... It seemed that my very soul tried in every way to leave the body's prison. But, on the other hand, I felt a desire to work for God, and the fear that through obedience I should not consent to die eventually brought my requests for heaven to an end, an exertion that caused me great distress. In fact, I was prohibited from desiring death and from asking the Lord for it."

so that I told her one time, 'In paradise you will share the merit and glory of the martyrs.' She replied humbly: 'To be a true martyr means that one suffers for the faith or another Christian virtue. Instead, I did not do a thing.'"

She was poor in spirit, in material things, and in attitude. Sister Filippin explains that "in her use of things, of money and clothing, she was always detached and poor. In her little room there was nothing except a rosary and a crucifix. She loved poverty and said that if poverty was the Spouse of Saint Francis, it was her spouse as well." Thus as she approached death, she repeated more than once to the sisters that she wanted to be buried in her most well-worn habit and that her coffin had to be made from certain boards that she had seen in the orchard, the leftover debris from aerial bombardments.

Humble, yet not insensitive to suffering, she was able to let injuries roll off her back. "So much so", adds Sister Filippin, "that once after having received a hard word from a sister, she commented, with me present: 'I pretended I did not hear it.' This was also one of the hidden gifts Bakhita had, which endeared her to so many people."

The examples of this sort are numerous. Sister Clotilde Sella recalls how another sister, Mother Margherita Zoccotti, told her the story about the time Bakhita traveled to the town of Soncino on behalf of the missions. The nun who accompanied her on this occasion gave her talk and then sent Bakhita up onto the stage insisting that she speak. Bakhita, however, "seemed confused, made the sign of the cross, and said, 'Be good, and love the Lord. See what favor he has shown to me.' Not knowing how to continue any further, she crossed herself and walked off the stage. The missionary nun scolded her sharply for having spoken too little. Bakhita, with humility and without losing her calm, apologized and thanked her. Witnessing this scene, Mother Margherita was so unnerved yet so moved by Bakhita's response that her humility made her weep."

She was poor in spirit and thus incredibly joyful, to such a degree that she was able to overlook any meanness or insult, even the more insignificant ones that typically foster some kind of resentment. "One day, I do not remember the circumstances," says Sister Angelina De Pretto, "she showed me something unusual—a piece of needlepoint with such bright colors that I blurted out, 'Oh, how ugly!' Smiling, Bakhita replied, 'I made it, you know!' I was left speechless both by my imprudent remark and her imperturbable serenity, and she gathered up her work and left as if she had received the highest compliment."

This humility in relation to others and to God sprang directly from her prayer life, to which, as we have seen, Bakhita dedicated many hours each day. Prayer and humility, which in the following episode, recounted by Sister Raccanello, shone forth in all their beauty.

In her final years, Bakhita was not able to walk by herself, which meant she had to wait for whoever was assigned the task of accompanying her to and fro. Sometimes it was the nurse on duty who would bring her to the chapel to pray, and then she would go back to her own chores. Mother Bakhita would stay there for hours. One of these times, passing by the chapel, I realized that she had been there since two in the afternoon (it was four-thirty at the time). I approached her and asked, "Mother, would you like me to take you back to your room?" Smiling, she replied, "No, thanks. If the nurse came and did not find me, she would think I needed to go out, and she would be displeased. Thank you, I am doing very well right here with our Lord. I do not have anything to do except pray for all of you, for sinners, for missionaries, and for the poor black people."

Hers was a life of poverty that she chose and sought to live out right to the end, as demonstrated in the following episode that Ida Zanolini brought forward during the beatification process.

"One day the superior was speaking about detachment and the spirit of poverty that a religious should have, and Mother Bakhita made the following statement: 'Mother, I do not have anything anymore. I do not have books because I see poorly now, and all the other things I have given away. I only have a rosary and a crucifix left, and if you would like, I will detach myself from them as well.' "

Indomitable in faith and in service to others

Bakhita's obedience and promptness to fulfill her superior's requests have become proverbial among the Canossians. The first sign of this availability (in part a holdover from her many years as a slave, but also the fruit of her gratitude and spirit of service) emerged in the house of catechumens in Venice where she decided to become a nun. To the superior who conveyed to her the difficulties, sacrifices, and obligations such a life involved, Bakhita gave a simple and immediate response: "I will do everything, just as long as I am told what it is."

Her availability was total. Her response to anyone who asked something of her was always yes. The sisters in her community were well aware of this quality, and it was sometimes hard for them to stop her from taking on so many things, for she would fulfill her own duties as well as those of others. We are well aware of this side of her character, too, having read the story of her life as a slave, and we are still amazed at how she never turned in rebellion or retaliation against any of those who daily treated her as a beast of burden and abused her.

Her own kidnappers took advantage of her obedience, for in order to steal her away without being noticed they asked her to get a bundle for them. As Bakhita put it: "I quickly obliged them and obeyed, as I always did with my mother." Similarly, when the Turkish general commanded her to appear before him in order to inflict the terrible injury of twisting her breasts, Bakhita said, "I ran to him and kneeled at his feet, awaiting his orders." This same scene was repeated twice again in the following days.

Such a display of submission is almost too much to countenance without feeling outraged. Bakhita provided only a partial explanation, recalling that she had witnessed other slaves with her who had died as a result of their rebellion, for it you did not obey, you were whipped. Nevertheless, one gets a clear sense that Bakhita's obedience was not merely a result of intimidation. She possessed an innate availability, which as a slave took the form of resignation that seemed to be waiting for better times.

The clear proof of all this took place when Bakhita, having changed her life, looked back and felt no resentment. On the contrary, she prayed for those who had kidnapped her, for those who had enslaved her, and for those who had abused her so badly that she was on the verge of death three times. To a sister who insisted on how malicious the people were who had done such evil to her, Bakhita replied: "Those poor souls were not bad; they did not know the good Lord and perhaps did not know how much harm they were doing to me. They were the masters, and I was their slave. Just as we are in the habit of doing good, the slave traders and owners did that out of habit, not out of wickedness."

At the same time we know how tenacious Bakhita was in pursuing the goal of baptism, the salvation of her soul, and her vocation to religious life. Tenacity, obedience, and a spirit of service were all bound together as one in her faith—a faith that was simultaneously simple and extraordinarily strong. In the house at Schio, all the nuns knew that as soon as the superior indicated some wish, Bakhita was ready to carry it out right away. "Though she had a number of different superiors, she was always ready to obey, for she saw the Lord in them", explains Sister Filippin. "When the superior speaks, it is God who is speaking", as Bakhita would say to those who asked her the reason why she was so available.[2] And not only did she practice obedience, but she encouraged the sisters to be obedient and available at all times, because "obedience pleases the Lord very much ... Whether healthy or suffering, one must always be obedient because this is the will of the Lord." Her conviction was so firm about this that she never asked to be excused from anything for reasons of health.

And Bakhita was obedient and available even when she would have preferred to direct her energies to other things. The following episode recounted by Sister Raccanello is one of the very few in which we glimpse Bakhita's obedience and availability vacillating momentarily, though she quickly recovered herself.

[2] Sister Dalla Costa recalled: "She did all she could, even to the point of guessing what her superiors and the other sisters wished, and she was ready and happy to fulfill it. She never rushed, however, and she scolded us when out of haste we neglected something."

"One time two boys came to the convent asking to see Mother Bakhita. It was three in the afternoon during the summer. The superior told me to suggest to Mother Bakhita that she come down, if she felt up to it. By that time she was already ill. At first she registered a little astonishment, saying, 'At this hour?' It was the only time her conduct surprised me, but she quickly let it go. She apologized and immediately put herself at their disposal. She joined the boys in the parlor and spoke with them at length without showing signs of weariness."

Bakhita's obedience, however, left her totally free to witness to the truth, even if it sometimes hurt and even if the person on the listening end was the superior. Such was the case when Mother Maria Martini, superior at Schio, asked for prayers because she was beset with many financial and material worries and was feeling desperate (this was during the Second World War). Bakhita listened and then, instead of taking the road of human consolation, she chose to deliver a sharp exhortation on trust in God: "But Mother, are you surprised that the Lord sends you tribulations? If he does not come to us with a little suffering, to whom is he supposed to go? Did we not join the convent in order to do his will? Yes, Mother, I will certainly pray a great deal, but so that his will may be done."

The challenge of being black

Bakhita faced the racial climate of her day with the same sense of pride with which she witnessed to the faith, exhorting people to follow the will of God. It should be kept in mind that in a place like northern Italy at the end of the nineteenth and beginning of the twentieth century, black people were seen only on postcards, in colonial propaganda books, in advertisements for exotic products or circus shows, on labels for shoe polish or those for soaps and bleaches claiming to turn even Africans white.

This was not an environment of outright racism but, rather, one of both ignorance and mistrust that manifested itself in various forms. One night, for example, during the First World War, the police encountered her on the street together with her superior, and they took Bakhita for a spy. Only after extensive explanations did the police decide not to put them both in jail.

We have already had occasion to describe how Bakhita was able to transform an unhealthy curiosity about her skin color into an instrument of evangelization. One might say that it was often precisely due to how different she looked (both because of her race and because of how she dressed) that she was able to appeal even to the hardest hearts, convinced as she was of the fact that God cares, not about the color of his children's skin, but about their ability to love.

So when the word spread in Schio that the portress at the Canossian convent was a black nun, many showed up at the front door merely out of curiosity. It was a curiosity that Bakhita had to put up with for the rest of her life and to which she often responded by making a witty wisecrack. Sister Maria Luisa Dagnino, in particular, remembers the time in 1938 when she went with Bakhita and Sister Benetti to a meeting on behalf of the missions. "On the train[3]

[3] In the context of train rides, the following episode is worth mentioning, as told by Sister Walburga Ricchieri: "I had to make a trip to Noventa Padovana. I got on the train with Mother Bakhita and a little black girl, Natalina Cortese, a schoolgirl at the house in Mirano. Upon seeing two black persons, the passengers let out a cry of astonishment. They thought the little one was Mother Bakhita's daughter and that I was a missionary who had

a woman asked Sister Benetti how long Bakhita had been in Italy. Sister Benetti replied, 'Fifty years.' Then the woman remarked, 'In fifty years the palms of her hands have become white.' At this, Bakhita joined the conversation and, pointing to the back of her hands, said, 'In another fifty years they will be white here as well.' "

But it was not only the people she met outside the convent who made comments about her skin color. It was also her own religious sisters and the priests who came to hear her confession and say Mass. The refrain was more or less always the same, halfway between humor and irony: "How do you manage to do it, Mother, with such dark hands to make such snow-white embroidery?" or, when as sacristan she was in charge of the white altar linens: "How do you keep the cloth so clean with those dark hands of yours?" Bakhita replied with patience, giving no heed to the racial allusions (which nonetheless must have weighed upon the heart of a woman who for a long time had not dared to ask if she could become a nun because it did not seem possible to her that a black woman would be allowed to do so). Her responses, too, always sounded the same, full of humility and submission to the will of God: "The Lord wanted it this way, and it cannot be changed." Or, calling attention to the equal dignity that every human being shares in God's eyes and to the shared purity received at baptism: "What counts is that one's soul is white."

With one of the orphans who was a boarder at the Schio house, Bakhita discussed this question with some added

---

ransomed them. We smiled and then answered their inquisitive questions with dignity. Bakhita told them some of her story, and, seeing how moved they were, she asked me: 'Mother, please permit me to give these gentlemen some religious medals . . .' They received these small gifts with religious devotion and with words of heartfelt gratitude."

emphasis: "Remember, little girl, that what is black here is not dirty. What is dirty is the sin of one's soul. So take care never to do that, because I see in your eyes that the Lord is asking something of you."

Immigrant with a gift for dialogue

If with her beatification Bakhita became a clear sign for Africa, today there are many in Italy who believe that with her canonization the Sudanese saint can become a model and sign of hope for immigrants who live in Europe. One who definitely shares this opinion is Father Paolo Serra, a Comboni missionary who runs a shelter for Africans in Rome: "Until now, all those in Italy and Europe who are involved with the issue of African immigration never thought about it. But Bakhita could very well become a reference point and inspiration for many. Bakhita's example could awaken a powerful sense of hope among the Sudanese who are here among us, and her canonization is a golden opportunity that we cannot let slip through our fingers."

In fact, there are shelters in Italy whose entire approach is based upon the example of Bakhita. One of these is a center called Migrantes Giuseppina Bakhita di Alba, in the province of Cuneo. Sixty volunteers work in this center, offering a wide range of assistance, including social and educational programs, shelter, medical and pharmaceutical care, faith formation, and opportunities for interreligious dialogue. This center began in 1992, the year of Bakhita's beatification. The director, Father Paolo Rocca, explains that "we decided to name it after Bakhita because it seemed that her own experience—coming from an animist background, then living in a Muslim culture and, finally, in a

Christian culture—would facilitate dialogue with the African people and make it easier. Also, Bakhita came to Italy as an immigrant. Therefore, she seemed to be a perfect example and model, a bridge that would enable dialogue. Looking back after nearly a decade, I can say that it was an excellent choice. We have never lacked financial assistance. Many graces have come to us. Personally, I have received an incredible one, but I cannot talk about it. Bakhita has been a real revelation."

Father Rocca continues, "The people who come through our doors take to Bakhita with fondness, especially those from Senegal and the Ivory Coast. We hand out images of Bakhita, holy cards and other material about her life. We aim to make her widely known. Above all, among the African women, for whom Bakhita carries special significance and becomes a sign of freedom. We have put her name in Arabic upon the door of the room dedicated to prayer, where anyone can pray according to his own faith, and the Muslims have never had any objection to this."

Another migrant center dedicated to Bakhita is located in Florence. Here the director of the office for immigrants and refugees is Father Mioli, a Scalabrini priest, who remembers hearing about Bakhita when he was in the minor seminary during World War II. "I was in Valdagno in the province of Vicenza," he recalls, "and when as a boy I returned home in the summer, I remember that people often spoke about Bakhita. What they were saying had the ring of sanctity to it."

The ways in which Bakhita's holiness makes itself known throughout the world, among people of all ages, places, and walks of life, have always been mysterious. One of the most interesting examples is the Bakhita-Follereau Group, which was founded in Turin in 1992. The group's aim is threefold: to help make the cultures of the southern hemisphere better known; to work on behalf of those who suffer from leprosy; and to spread the message of Raoul Follereau (1903–1977), the internationally known advocate for lepers, and of Saint Josephine Bakhita. In partnership with the diocese of Turin, the group enjoys the active collaboration of the young people in the city and those in many surrounding schools in the Piedmont region. The directors of the group are Silvana Bottignole, Father Fabrizio Fassino, and Marco Paccò. They publish a magazine called *Bakhita News*, with information on the group's activities around the world. Two phrases stand out on its cover: "You will bring people peace only by enriching their hearts" (Raoul Follereau) and "Take heart, I am praying for you" (Bakhita). She is also presented as a "luminous figure of a non-EU immigrant in Italy".

The Follereau–Bakhita Group has launched and supports projects in Cape Verde, India, Zimbabwe, Brazil, and Sudan. The Group organizes an annual poetry prize for young people between eighteen and twenty-five years old, called "The Bakhita Competition: We Poets". With the youth the group also organizes theatrical events as well as encounters with important cultural, religious, and social figures. In Cape Verde a sister organization bearing the same name has been founded along with a treatment center for lepers. In the town of Warangal, in Andhra Pradesh in India, the group has helped start the Nava Jivan (new life) treatment center, which was opened on December 22, 1996, by Giovanni Cardinal Saldarini, bishop of Turin. This center helps to offer as well as to find employment both for those who once suffered from leprosy and for disabled persons. Inside the center, a place of particular devotion has been created: a small altar dedicated to Bakhita.

Silvana Bottignole, a psychologist who is also the editor of *Bakhita News*, explains that "the young people like Bakhita a lot. And not only them. I was pleased to discover at a recent event in Turin that Rigoberta Menchù (the Nobel Peace Prize winner) and the Nigerian writer Wole Soyinka (also a Nobel Prize winner) are both fond of Bakhita. Soyinka, in particular, told me that he is sure she is a great saint."

A missionary forever

"I want to fly in order to reach everyone and enlighten them about the faith, because there are few missionaries, and Africa is big", Bakhita declared in conversation with Sister Dalla Costa. This same sister recorded that Mother Josephine "desired to go to heaven because then she would be able to rouse the Lord to help the Africans and her relatives."

These are lines that beautifully express the missionary spirit that moved Bakhita from the very moment she received the gift of faith and understood that what had happened to her could in fact affect the destiny of her relatives and the history of Africa. She possessed a keen awareness of being a missionary in and through prayer. She intuited—or perhaps she understood very precisely, since we are unable to plumb the depths of the mystery of holiness, nor can we grasp the prophetic capacities of the saints—that even though she lived a simple and, in many ways, obscure life of a nun in a little northern Italian town, despite all of this she could truly bring Christ to the world, "raising up a people to God" in her Africa. Unwavering faith and incessant prayer were her resources, and she knew how to use them and how powerful they are.

Such convictions were evident in the following episode recounted by Sister Irma Riva, which refers back to the time when Bakhita served as portress in 1938 at the school for foreign missions in Vimercate (Lombardy): "Sister Bakhita saw me come through the door in tears because I had been sent back to the novitiate in Venice. I was told that my health was not robust enough for the foreign missions. This was Bakhita's response: 'Take heart, you and I will become saints and missionaries from where we are right here, and we will save many souls.' She said this to me in such a matter of fact way that I was filled with much consolation and comfort."

In Africa and around the world

Bakhita's great desire to reach every corner of the globe and to help her African continent is translated into concrete reality year by year, and with an intensity that continues to gather momentum. And it is worth noting how devotion to Bakhita (with its accompanying fruits) is spreading at an extraordinary rate, yet in a way that is completely natural and spontaneous.

We have already mentioned how instrumental the members of Opus Dei have been in making Bakhita known to the world. But this work of promotion would have been in vain had Bakhita's holiness not been so attractive, striking a powerful chord in people's hearts today. Otherwise, the 250,000 followers of Escrivá who arrived from around the world in Saint Peter's Square for the double beatification would not have taken notice of Bakhita, just as nobody noticed the few hundred Africans present on that day, who were easily overlooked (by the mass media) and then disappeared within the huge Opus Dei crowd.

If today, such a short time after that event in Rome, one can count across the globe over a hundred chapels, parishes, prayer groups and youth groups, base communities, hospitals, health centers and medical dispensaries, schools, and at least two religious communities bearing the name of Bakhita, then there must be something exceedingly attractive and prophetic about this humble black nun who was once a slave.

In Africa, devotion to Bakhita is growing exponentially, also in areas far from Canossian missions. In fact, in some cases, it is not so much the missions run by the daughters and sons of Magdalene of Canossa who are making Bakhita known; rather, it is the African saint who is helping the Canossians make inroads in mission territory.

"People feel that she is their friend", emphasizes Sister Maria Lucia Tokoyo, the Comboni missionary from Congo. "And they see her as a model to follow in their journey of faith. For all of us, Bakhita is proof that a daughter of Africa can become a symbol for the whole world. Just have a look— Bakhita embodies the dignity of Africa for all mankind to see. Africans recognize this and feel it with a sense of pride and as a sign of hope."

Indeed, it is a two-pronged hope: hope in the abilities and gifts of Africans; hope in the possibility of dialogue, of constructive coexistence and brotherhood with the West.

Sister Maria Lucia adds:

Bakhita bears witness to the fact that there are people of goodwill in Europe who are truly committed to helping Africa. If this were not the case, she would not have been ransomed from slavery or welcomed in Italy, later to return as a saint to Africa. Bakhita is living proof that the relationship between Europe and Africa is not simply one of oppressor and oppressed. Bakhita is a sign of what unites Europeans and Africans. Blessed Comboni always said that Jesus also died for the Africans and that they are children of

God. Today we take this for granted, but Bakhita fulfilled this reality for Africa. She is a symbol of this achievement.

For the Congolese nun, but also for all religious, African and Western alike, who work in areas where the Sudanese saint is well known, the proof of this can be seen in the innumerable unbidden ways in which devotion to Bakhita has spread. They are so simple and natural that many times, as several Comboni and Xaverian missionaries have observed, all one has to do is look around at the local geography to see, for example, that the center for women's rights one just visited is dedicated to Bakhita, that the nearby parish has a chapel or prayer group dedicated to Bakhita, that choirs at Mass are singing about Bakhita.

And all of this has occurred without the Church in Africa having exerted any particular effort to promote the saint. Thus Bakhita's great desire to make the love of God known among the African people is quietly yet steadily coming to fruition. Sister Maria Lucia continues:

> I have thought about this many times, and I have come to the only possible explanation. Bakhita's success stems from the fact that she is a key historical figure for Africa. Bakhita bears within her the whole history of Africa, ancient and modern: slavery, exploitation, the West, the missions, colonization, Islam, the problems and discrimination faced by women, the search for freedom, the possibility of dialogue with Europe... There is no other way to account for so much devotion to her beyond the borders of Sudan. In Congo, Bakhita's presence is tremendous, even in the eastern regions and in the diocese of Isiro, where Blessed Anuarite died a martyr in 1964. There, where the memory of Anuarite is extremely strong and where a shrine to this local saint has been erected, devotion to Bakhita is enormous.

As it is in Congo, so it is in Uganda, Tanzania, and Kenya. In these countries, since the 1980s, many religious orders of women give to the girls who are considering a religious vocation books about Bakhita's life in French, English, and the local language. In Lubumbashi, in southern Congo, a congregation of men was recently started that bears Bakhita's name. In Mtoni, on the outskirts of the Tanzanian capital of Dar es Salaam, we find a parish dedicated to the Sudanese saint that even has its own website. Churches named after Bakhita can also be found in Malawi, Sierra Leone, Cameroon, Togo, Ghana, and elsewhere. As mentioned earlier, a huge painting of the smiling Bakhita hangs in the cathedral of Nairobi, Kenya.

In the Kenyan town of Kitale, between the capital and the Sudanese border, one can visit the Bakhita Information Center, which for several years now has also run a school for vocations and faith formation as well as for elementary schoolteachers and catechists. Also in Nairobi one can find another beautiful image of Bakhita in the parish dedicated to Our Lady of Guadalupe, run by Mexican missionaries.

This latter example is a sign of the role Bakhita is also playing in Latin America. And not only in Mexico. In Brazil a miracle took place (we discuss it at length in the section on miracles and answered prayers) that was instrumental in Bakhita's canonization. Also in Brazil, within several communities that gather for popular Christian-syncretistic celebrations, Bakhita has come to replace the figure of the slave Isaura, because the Sudanese nun is an ex-slave who became a saint. In Argentina, in the Italian hospital in the city of La Plaza, a chapel dedicated to Bakhita has become the place where those in need of material or spiritual help all come to pray.

Devotion to Bakhita is also growing in the United States, in particular within African-American communities. We can witness this, for example, in the Basilica of the National

Shrine of the Immaculate Conception in Washington, D.C., where a relic of Saint Bakhita has been placed in the altar of the Our Mother of Africa Chapel.

One day the Lord will set us free

"Bakhita is a symbolic figure, and with humility I feel close to this African saint whose soul has been shaped by the Lord for our times." When Bernardin Cardinal Gantin spoke about the Sudanese nun, he closed his eyes as if inspired, and his face became radiant.[4] "Bakhita", he said, "is the person who inhabits my meditation. I turn to her when facing the most important events in my life and for Africa. Bakhita ... Josephine Bakhita. Joseph was also uneducated, he was humble, but he was the teacher of Jesus ... Marvelous."

Born in 1922 in Toffo, in the diocese of Cotonou, Benin, Bernardin Gantin was ordained a priest in 1951 and went on to serve the Church as prefect of the Congregation for Bishops (1984–1998) and as dean of the College of Cardinals (1993–2002). Cardinal Gantin died in 2008. His love for the black continent was at least as great as the pain and anger he experienced as a result of the political, economic, religious, and social tragedies and injustices that overwhelm his people every day. His indignation was clearly visible in the lines of his face as well as in his words of social criticism: "Ours is a very sad reality. We are oppressed, trampled upon, exploited every day for oil, for diamonds ... And then there are the cruel dictators who rule us, Africans who are unable to grow, who kill each other in a spiral of violence and hatred that seems endless."

[4] As a result of Cardinal Gantin's personal initiative, the diocese of Cotonou recently built a church dedicated to Josephine Bakhita.

It is within this dramatic context that Gantin situates Bakhita's prophetic power:

> All the historical tragedies of the continent converge in her and are recapitulated, relived. Torn away from her people, sold, resold, and sold again ... And yet nobody even raped her—a sign of God's love for her and for all of us.
>
> When I went to Schio, I prayed for a long time at her tomb. Bakhita reminded me of my mother; she made me understand the huge role that women can play in Africa today. For it is not by chance that, in order to show us the way to freedom, of redemption, the Lord specifically chose a woman. African women have always been exploited. But in Bakhita, an African woman whose history is our history, the people discover a beacon of hope. She who never asked anybody for anything has obtained everything. She, a black woman who belonged to everyone, is loved by all, by Africans and Europeans alike, by Americans as well as Asians. She is a little star capable of illuminating the entire world.
>
> I believe that Bakhita is a great symbol. A concrete symbol. The certainty that one day the Lord will set us free. A sign and a commitment for Italy, too, the country that ransomed her and welcomed her as its own daughter.

Sudan, land of suffering

We have seen on many levels that between the Sudan of Bakhita's day and the Sudan of today very few differences exist. The regime[5] imposed Islamic law and for decades has

[5] In this context, it is worth repeating what has already been noted: the political landscape in Sudan has changed dramatically since the publication of the Italian edition of this book in 2000. In 2005 the twenty-two-year civil war in Sudan ended, and on July 9, 2011, South Sudan became an independent democratic state, not ruled by Islamic law.— Trans.

been engaged in a civil war that has been fought with every possible weapon, including extermination by famine, between the Muslim North and the Christian and animist South. It is a religious and ethnic war: black African populations live in the South, while the North has been largely Islamified. In such a situation, ancient strategies for subjecting others are perpetuated: children are kidnapped in order to make them slaves and concubines or to turn them into soldiers used against their very own villages.

This all unfolds within a delicate political and economic context in a country that is a natural crossroads between the traditionally unstable region of the Horn of Africa and the pro-Western nation of Egypt; or between the pan-Arab myth of Libya and the strong Western interest (in oil, diamonds, and rare minerals) within Sudan itself and its bordering countries to the west and south.

This is a very difficult world, and Bakhita is becoming a point of reference in it for the Christians and blacks who are subjected to all sorts of harassment and oppression. This is true, above all, for the ever-growing population of refugees who are crowding around Khartoum. People who flee from the South and then walk for hundreds, even thousands of miles on foot, often losing elderly family members, the weak, and babies along the way, until they finally reach the periphery of the capital. Here the government very often rounds up these refugees and transports them to the North, into the Nubian desert. After a few years, when villages and large swaths of mud huts mushroom up around a little church, a missionary, and a little agricultural activity, then the bulldozers arrive, manned by government troops, who raze everything to the ground, forcing people to move and begin again from scratch.

The predicament of Christians and non-Muslims in general is dire. In order to grasp their plight it is enough to listen to the rhetoric of Hassan al-Turabi, the regime's Islamist ideologue, writing in his *Dialogue with the West*: "It is fundamental for us to change the Western world's vision of Islam. We Muslims need to dialogue and communicate our message according to our effective fundamentalistic, experiential, and deductive method in order to modernize our position as 'agents' of Allah. This involves a gradual plan in the general context of comprehension, universality, and integration of Islam as *sharia* [Islamic law], belief, civilization, and a universal way of life. Our victory and the aim of the battle is to preach to others that they must subject themselves to the will of Allah."

Eloquent words which, by way of comparison, evoke an equally eloquent rebuttal from the Comboni missionary Father Renato (Kizito) Sesana: "When it is not using bombs and raids, Khartoum's army makes use of famine and the refugees themselves as weapons for decimating the populations of the South. But it is also true that many leaders of the various Sudanese factions (some supported by the United States) bear responsibility for how they treat their own people. These are corrupt and manipulated men who control their regions with arrogance, imposing absurdly high taxes, hoarding humanitarian aid, and seeking to extort money from volunteer organizations and from the Church."

This is the sort of tragedy that plays out across much of Africa. It is a situation that comes to light in all its crude and frankly embarrassing reality through the words of Bishop Macram Max Gassis, bishop of El Obeid, drawn from his Christmas Prayer in 1999:

While the world is preoccupied with mundane plans,
My people cries out: *Save us, O Lord, we are going to drown.*
My people cries out to be saved from *jihad*, the Islamic
  holy war.

My people cries out to be saved from rape.

My people cries out to be saved from air raids and minefields.

My people cries out to be saved from slavery.

My people cries out to be saved from famine created by man.

My people cries out to be saved from those who claim to speak for what we need and for our priorities.

My people cries out to be saved from those who destroy the unity of the Church and of Sudan.

My people cries out to be saved from those who under the guise of fatigue commiserate with us but refuse to offer us assistance and solidarity.

Lord, as we celebrate your birth at the beginning of a new millennium, we humbly ask:

That our brother bishops listen to us as voices that have no voice ...

That priests and their communities join together with their bishops in order to come to our aid.

That the leaders of the Christian nations may be inspired by the Holy Spirit and commit themselves to putting an end to the suffering in Sudan ...

That people of goodwill may continue to help us in the process of healing and reconciliation.

Lord Jesus, we thank you for the gift of the first Sudanese saint, Josephine Bakhita.

She too was sold, bought, and ransomed.

From the bitterness and shame of earthly slavery, she freely became a slave of Your Love.

May she intercede for her brothers and sisters so that they may be saved from the evil of slavery and from those who have given up on the redemption of her people.

May she obtain for the Church and for Sudan the gift of justice and peace. Amen.

In one of the enormous villages made up of refugees from the South, suspended between life and death, about eighteen miles from Khartoum stands a small ramshackle church constructed out of scrap material. In large part it is portable, ready to be reassembled when government forces come and knock it to the ground. Inside this little church, behind the altar, three large murals are displayed upon the structure's only real wall, made of mud-and-straw bricks. On the left, the baptism of Bakhita is depicted within a desert setting, reflecting the landscape surrounding the village,[6] complete with the Holy Spirit descending upon her in the likeness of a dove. In the middle, a large mural features the smiling face of Mother Josephine. And on the right, also painted by hand, is an image of our Lady, next to the Sacred Heart of Jesus.

This city in the form of a village is called Jabarona, with nearly seventy thousand inhabitants. The church, dedicated to Bakhita, serves a parish covering a vast area, which includes numerous similar centers, making up a total of a million persons, all refugees from the South. The parish priest is Father Mark. A huge piazza spreads out in front of the church, with an altar and a large wooden cross, which is used for outdoor celebrations. In back, upon a wall of multicolored bricks, one finds a large portrait of Bakhita next to the logo of the Jubilee Year 2000.

Father Mark is a robust Sudanese priest from the diocese of Khartoum. He has great admiration for Bakhita, and his devotion to her is deep, "like that of all the people who

---

[6] In many cases, the African culture has adapted episodes from Bakhita's life story.

live here", he explains. "Bakhita is considered one who loves the poor and the young. Boys and girls see her as the model of the new Church. The people think and talk about her as if she were living in our midst, and they say that when they pray to 'Our Mother Bakhita' many problems are resolved. In our refugee camps, there are schools dedicated to Bakhita, and there is a plan to construct another church bearing her name in the middle of the desert."

Christians in the South identify with Bakhita, and through her inspiration they are able to continue their daily struggles against hunger and discrimination. But what is most extraordinary is that Bakhita's presence has begun to facilitate dialogue between Christians and Muslims. Father Mark explains that this occurs on a daily basis. "Bakhita", he says, "has a tremendous appeal among young people, and she is loved by the less intransigent Muslims. One could say that Bakhita is playing an important role in the dialogue between African Muslims and Christians, because everyone respects her. Bakhita's story has become a great challenge, provoking much discussion and pointing toward a renewed missionary and catechetical outreach in Africa. She is arousing a new spirit in many local churches, leading to numerous vocations and fostering a renewed respect for the European missionaries."

The Comboni missionary Father Ramanzini also testifies to the renewal that is stirring within the Church in Sudan:

From the moment the Pope "brought Bakhita back" to Sudan in February 1993, the Church here has been experiencing enormous graces. The fact that the Pope came for Sudan and for Bakhita has set the hearts of Christians ablaze. So many parents name their daughters Bakhita. Along with Father Mark's church, every one of the twenty-five parishes in the diocese has at least one side-chapel that bears the name of Bakhita. In Khartoum there is an association of university students that has adopted her name as have so many communities and prayer centers for vocations as well as charity organizations. Every February 8, Bakhita's feast day, the stadium at Comboni College in Khartoum is filled to maximum capacity for the celebration and festivities. There are books in Arabic and English about her life. There is a small theater group of young people who frequently put on plays about her life, emphasizing above all the fact that her slavery led her to God and to the awareness that she is a daughter, free and loved forever.

Father Ramanzini makes a point of underscoring how this spiritual awakening is gathering force among Sudanese women most of all.

Devotion to Bakhita is spreading in simple and spontaneous ways. It is as if Bakhita's roots had always remained in Sudan and the only thing they needed in order to blossom once more was a little rainfall. Prayers of intercession to Bakhita for the salvation of Sudan are a commonplace at Masses and other liturgical celebrations. And her positive impact upon Christian women can be seen in their commitment and search for spiritual strength that will help them shoulder their everyday experiences of pain, loneliness, oppression, and the injustices that stem from the political, social, and religious situation in this country without peace.

There are many forms of oppression suffered by Sudanese women, and especially South Sudanese women, which mirror Bakhita's experience in her own day. They lack a permanent residence or home; they are constantly moving; subjected to Islamic law, their dignity is demeaned; their respect and family honor is trampled upon. Christian women see in Bakhita a powerful role model for living their faith in these stifling circumstances. Following in Bakhita's foot-steps, they rediscover their own sense of dignity, which enables them to overcome despair and to hope in a better future. Thus, it is clear as daylight that it is only with this kind of patience that Christian Sudanese women are able to survive these conditions. Traditional African patience alone cannot account for courage such as this.

A song for Africa

Going to Mass in Jabarona or in any of the Catholic chap-els scattered throughout Sudan is an unforgettable experi-ence. It is so different from most of our Western Sunday Masses that it can barely be described or understood with-out seeing it for oneself. Every gesture, every word is imbued with a palpable sense that the faith and trust and courage to meet the challenges of the day, and maybe even those of tomorrow, are gifts that we receive as God's children. The songs, too, make a profound impression, even upon those who are passing the church by chance, perhaps for the first and last time. For an unmistakable sense of childlike faith flows through the joyful rhythms, verses, and refrains of each song.

And the new songs about Bakhita multiply year after year. They are transmitted from community to community sim-ply by singing, literally by word of mouth, in the purest African tradition. And not only in Sudan, but also in Congo, Uganda, Zimbabwe, and elsewhere. It almost seems that, little by little, all of Africa wants to begin singing about Bakhita. Little by little, as with "I'm Going Slowly, Slowly toward Eternity", one of the most well-known songs about the Sudanese saint, which presents the anecdote about the two suitcases.

The refrain of this song, set to music by the Jesuit priest
Jean Jacques Luzitu Mukunda, goes like this:

> I'm going slowly, slowly toward Eternity.
> I'm carrying two suitcases, slowly slowly.
> One of them has all my sins inside,
> the other one, the heavy one,
> That one has the merits of Christ inside.

In the three stanzas, the people ask Bakhita about what she
will do when she comes before God, and Bakhita replies:

> When I come before the throne of God,
> I'll simply cover my ugly suitcase
> with the merits of our Lady.
> And then, slowly, slowly,
> I'll tell the Father Almighty:
> "Please judge me according to what you see."

> When I come before the love of God,
> I'll simply show our Father
> all the merits of Jesus Christ.
> And then, slowly, slowly,
> I'll tell him with a smile:
> "This is the gift that your daughter is carrying."

> When I come before the tenderness of God,
> I'm certain that I won't be turned away
> because God is so rich in mercy.
> And that's why, slowly, slowly,
> I'll turn to Saint Peter and say:
> "You can close the gate—I'm here to stay."

The refrain of another song is noteworthy, too, for it tells about the great power of Bakhita's message:

> Bakhita, daughter of Africa,
> we give thanks for your life
> that shines like a bright star
> and shows the way for all of Africa.
> Bakhita, daughter of the whole world.

. In a third song, the people are complaining to God about life's infinite hardships, and Bakhita's voice responds in the refrain with the following invitation:

> Join with me in prayer to the Lord,
> who has freed me from every chain.
> My name is "Lucky"—Bakhita!
> Join with me in prayer to the Lord.

"There is certainly a reason why the first Sudanese saint bears the name of Bakhita-Lucky", wrote the archbishop of Khartoum, Gabriel Zubier Waco, to the people of Sudan on the occasion of the Pope's visit. And the archbishop reveals the reason in his prayer of hope and reconciliation:

All of you who are refugees, oppressed, exhausted, and without a roof—you are "Bakhita". All of you who are victims of injustice and exploitation, victims of discrimination and of persecution—you are "Bakhita". And God's love and tenderness embrace you.

You are unable to understand this now, but you will discover it later; you will certainly discover it. God will never betray you. Bakhita understood this and experienced God's saving power. She prayed for everyone, and she will never stop praying for you, oppressors and oppressed alike, both masters and slaves, persecutors and persecuted.

Even you—those of you who oppress your brothers and sisters, who govern without justice and without shame, stepping upon the bodies of others as if they were grass—even you are "Bakhita". You who are so blind to your egoism that you are unable to see the urgent needs of your brothers and sisters. Bakhita has also prayed for you, that God will forgive you.

From the hands of our one and only God, the loving Father of all, we receive grace upon grace, an overflowing of love, joy, and hope that will pour out across our land. Bakhita will pray that this may come true. She has not forgotten you!

VIII

The Great Book of Miracles

There are many memorable phrases and anecdotes in Bakhita's life that are cited with frequency. There are some, however, such as, "Take heart, I will pray for you", that possess universal scope and meaning, that have a way of connecting with the deepest human and spiritual sentiments: from tenderness to hope to suffering. These are words that express a promise and a powerful guarantee of faithfulness. Words that people can immediately understand and take to heart, even before they read them in Bakhita's biographies. Words that are legible in the smile on her face, in her life's journey, in what people have said about her, in things that have happened thanks to her presence, in her extraordinary openness and availability, in her sympathy and compassion. Words that receive daily confirmation in the helps and graces and miracles that come through her intercession.

The official miracles

By official miracles we mean those that were selected to promote her causes for beatification and canonization. In order to proclaim someone a saint or a blessed, the Church requires, among other things, documented proof of a miracle obtained through his intercession. Usually this involves healings. To be considered miraculous, these healings must be proved to be scientifically unexplainable, and their enduring effects must also be proved by the most expert doctors in the field.

Two official miracles were proved in Bakhita's case. The first took place in Pavia, Italy, only eight months after her death, while the second occurred in Santos, Brazil, ten days after her beatification. The first involved the healing of a Canossian nun, the second a sixty-one-year-old maid, separated, with four children. Each healing was verified as instantaneous and as having taken place in the context of intense prayer.

In 1939, in the Canossian convent of Pavia, Mother Angela Silla Mari began to feel that first strong pain in her left knee, which swelled up and produced pus. The condition was accompanied by very high fevers. She was diagnosed with tubercular synovitis of the knee, and after a short time, due to consumptive cartilage, she completely lost the capacity to move her leg.

At Pavia's general hospital she was advised to undergo sun therapy, and in March 1940 she was admitted to the sun therapy center of Arma di Taggia. The regimen consisted of sun treatments, a balanced diet, calcium and iodine-arsenic injections, and physical therapy. Over the next eight months, pus was drawn from the leg 182 times. Three abscesses developed in the leg that secreted pus and that would heal and then open up again continuously until the day of the miraculous healing.

On July 11, 1944, by order of the German command, the hospital of Arma di Taggia was evacuated. Mother Angela was taken to her parents' home in Pieve di Coriano, where she stayed for several days. But the retreating Germans then blew up the bridges, forcing Mother Angela to stay with her parents for nearly a year, always in bed with pain and fever. In August 1945 she returned to Pavia. Her illness continued to get worse, resistant to all treatment. By now the kneecap and part of the shinbone were gravely compromised. In 1947 a well-known orthopedic surgeon from Genoa recommended removal of the kneecap and a portion of the shinbone.

The operation was scheduled for October 12 in Pavia under Giovanni Morone. On October 4, Mother Angela traveled to the hospital. While she was being admitted, Sister Rachele Ruggeri urged her to join her in a novena to Mother Bakhita, who had died eight months earlier with a reputation for sanctity.

Having completed all the necessary medical exams, on the evening of October 11 Doctor Angelo Massone medicated the knee and cleaned the abscesses in preparation for the operation the following morning. The patient prayed and slept very little during the night. On October 12 at 2 A.M., Mother Angela was awakened suddenly by a voice that said, "Wake up and walk." She felt a strong desire to get out of bed, and in astonishment she realized that she was able to do so by herself and without support. Mother Angela walked. She made a circle around the bed and then began to weep. Her first impulse was to thank Mother Bakhita. Then she took the pus-soaked bandages off her knee. The abscesses were gone, the swelling had disappeared, and there was no more pain.

In the morning, Doctors Morone and Capella, ready to perform the operation, visited their patient and were dumbfounded. They examined her, took new X-rays, and after consulting with each other they declared that an operation was unnecessary, for the knee was healed. The next day Mother Angela walked out of the hospital on two strong legs.

A completely different story altogether was the ordeal of Eva Da Costa. She was born in Iguape, in the state of São Paulo, Brazil, on January 1, 1931. At the age of twelve she left her family to earn a living as a maid and cleaning lady. At nineteen she married Yoziro Onishi, of Japanese origin. They had four children, two boys and two girls, who remained under Eva's care after a legal separation.

In order to care for her children and send them to school, Eva worked day and night, which posed a serious health risk for one who had already been diagnosed with diabetes mellitus. In 1976, while working at her job, she fell into a hyperglycemic coma. In 1990, while working for a company in the city of São Paulo, Eva felt the initial symptoms of a grave degenerative ailment that struck the right leg first and then the left leg: an intense burning sensation in the calf that over time turned her leg a livid blue.

Months passed, and where the burning was first felt, pus-filled wounds appeared, swelling the leg. Eva had little money and was beset with many family problems. She worked and had no time to seek medical attention. When her discomfort became intolerable, she went to the emergency room, where the medical attendant on duty prescribed ineffective cortisone cream. She later went to see the municipal doctor, who made the following diagnosis: eczema and mycotic dermatitis, with an underlying pathology of diabetes mellitus. Yet another doctor diagnosed her with "infected eczema". In 1991 the diagnosis of a specialist read as follows: "Infected ulcerations of the patient's lower limbs with chronic venous insufficiency, obesity, and high blood pressure." He recommended amputation of the right leg due to the detection of gangrene. The wounds on both legs were so bad that bone was visible.

Eva Da Costa was without hope. The creams she had purchased with her slim savings were useless, and in a moment of desperation she threw them away. She needed to go to the hospital but also needed to continue working out of necessity.

It was now April 1992. Eva did not realize it yet, but everything was about to change. On Friday the twenty-fourth, she received a visit from a nun of the Canossian community of Santos. Her name was Mother Regina dos Santos, and she was making the rounds in the neighborhood, visiting the sick people she knew. Eva welcomed her visit, told her all about her trials, and showed the nun her leg. Mother dos Santos was shocked. "Her calves", she reported later, "were horrible to look at, especially the wounds on her right leg that revealed the bone."

Mother Regina could think of nothing better than to invite Eva to the Wednesday prayer meetings in the cathedral organized by the Elderly Women's Group in preparation and thanksgiving for the beatification of Mother Josephine Bakhita. The eighty or more women in the group prayed a novena together every Wednesday from April 29 to June 24. At each meeting Mother Regina narrated several episodes from the life of the Sudanese nun, then recited the rosary and the intercessary prayer that is found, today as well as then, on the back of the holy cards of Bakhita.

Eva was not well and could not always participate. On May 27, however, she was able to go. The nun recounted the episodes in which Bakhita had been tortured: the beatings, the tattooing, the twisting of her breasts ... Eva Da Costa was so moved as she listened to the stories of Bakhita's suffering, so similar in many ways to her own, that her hands instinctively traveled down her leg, touching her wounds. In silence she made a humble prayer of petition:

"Bakhita, you who have suffered so much, please help me, and, for the love of God, make my legs get better."

As soon as she finished her prayer, the pain and burning sensation in her legs vanished. A shy and reserved person all her life, Eva did not say a word to anyone. When she returned home, however, her youngest son, Sidney, noticed that his mother was moving about without any difficulty. He asked her about it, and she told him what had happened when she was praying in the cathedral. Neither one attempted to explain what had taken place. Yet, over the next twenty-four hours, when Eva discovered that her wounds were healed and the skin had begun to cover her calves again, they realized that her recovery was a miracle.

On the following Wednesday, June 3, Eva returned to the cathedral for the novena. She waited until the meeting was over and then called Mother Regina aside, showing her both legs. The nun, who remembered well what she had beheld only a few weeks earlier, began to ask her questions but was pulled away by some other women who needed her at that moment.

Eva returned for the novena on the following Wednesday. The group of eighty or so women were there along with numerous other people who were in the cathedral by chance or who had come to hear about the newly beatified African. Also present that night was one of the general counselors of the Canossians, Sister Maria Luisa Leggeri, who spoke with fervor about Bakhita, her amazing life story, and the many graces and miracles throughout the world that had occurred through her intercession. Filled with confidence by these enthusiastic words, Eva Da Costa stood up, told her own story, and revealed her healed leg to everyone.

Conversions and graces

It would be impossible to recount in these pages the thousands of occasions in which our Lord has intervened directly in people's lives through Bakhita's prayers of intercession. The documentation related to her cause for beatification already contained hundreds of cases in Italy alone. Every day, however, letters arrive at the various Canossian houses spread throughout the world, detailing ongoing cases of graces received. These direct interventions from heaven are also reported by Comboni missionaries and others across the globe who have had the good fortune to know about Bakhita. We have recounted a number of these stories here already, and we have seen that they involve not only healings but also concrete manifestations of help in resolving tangled family and employment situations, aid in finding a job as well as in completing work-related tasks, significant spiritual interventions, conversions, direct manifestations of God's love, confirmations of faith, vocations, capacity for discernment, a deepening of one's love for the Church and one's community.

A great number of favors have been granted to people who were completely unaware that someone was praying for them. One such case was described by Maria Pozzan about a woman in Schio who confided in a Canossian nun the sorrow she felt because her husband was far away from the faith. The nun counseled her to place a holy card of Bakhita under her husband's pillow. That very night the man had a dream about Bakhita smiling and gesturing to him with her hands. The following night he dreamed the same thing again. So he told his wife about it, wondering what on earth the Little Brown Mother could want from him. His wife answered: "She wants your conversion." The man decided on the spot to go to confession, and, as Pozzan made a point of noting, "he still goes to this day."

The following story is one about a physical healing, presented by the municipal doctor of Schio, Massimino Bertoldi, who was also Bakhita's own doctor in the final years of her life. The healing involved Doctor Bertoldi's daughter, who for months had been recovering from unsuccessful abdominal surgery in the Milan City hospital (in the year 1953–1954). Internal stitches had caused an infection, and, despite all treatments, her fever did not decrease and her clinical situation worsened. Doctor Bertoldi, on the occasion of a medical visit to the Canossian house on Via Fusinato, spoke with the mother superior, who advised him to give his daughter a holy card of Bakhita as well as a relic that she should place on her abdomen and to pray ardently. "My daughter", the doctor recalled, "followed this advice, and on the very same day the fever left her. The surgeon removed the drainage tube, and the wound began to heal, becoming firm from the bottom upward until it closed. And so it remains to this day. The surgeon who was attending her, seeing the situation change so rapidly, said: 'It seems almost like a miracle.' After a period of time it was determined that the wound was completely healed."

Doctor Bertoldi himself became quite ill later and was healed of throat cancer (he had been a heavy smoker). His wife, Constantina, told the sisters that this healing was a result of her prayers asking for Bakhita's intercession.

Sister Clotilde Sella described how her little eight-year-old cousin was rushed to the emergency room in Schio with an abscess on her right hip and another on her left leg. She was operated on, but even after a month there were no signs of improvement. Instead, her fever rose, and the infection continued to spread. "I went to her myself," she recalled "and I brought with me a little piece of Bakhita's clothing. I sewed it into the back of my cousin's little blouse, because she could not sit upright, and I urged her to say three Glory Be's to Mother Bakhita before going to sleep. The next morning the girl was already sitting up in bed, and in a very short time she was perfectly healed."

On a less serious note, there is the story of Sister Teresa Martini, mother superior of the Schio house, who several months after Bakhita's death became almost completely deaf due to old age as well as an ear infection. All the sisters in the house began a novena, while Sister Martini placed a holy card with a relic of Bakhita to her ear. The result: she recovered her hearing, which remained strong to the day she died, years later. Then there is the story of the sudden healing from a case of kidney stones; then there was the healing of the baby with heart problems and the story of the Muslim who converted, and . . .

It is pointless to go on and on. God has chosen to touch countless lives—and history itself—through Bakhita in these decades that straddle the twentieth and twenty-first centuries. God's hand has been at work through the Sudanese saint in a particularly intense and constant way that is destined to continue bearing fruit in Italy and in Africa and around the world. This seems clear from the little that this book has managed to narrate and document. So much more remains hidden in people's hearts, to say nothing of events that take place every day and that go undocumented.

The roads of conversion and grace often remain mysterious and completely unknown. Just like the mysterious attraction of a poor, uneducated, barely literate, African nun. Mystery and attraction. The certainty of being loved and of being led by the hand to know the infinite mercy of the *Paròn*. This is the love (as we saw at the very outset) that is sought with such childlike faith and fervor in the letters, postcards, photographs, messages, invocations, and cries of suffering and of hope left beneath Bakhita's pillow each day in her room in Schio.

ACKNOWLEDGMENTS

I would like to thank the following people for their valuable information:

Elide De Liberali
Domenico Perozzo
Monsignor Antonio Casieri
Father Giuseppe Farina
Sister Giulia Pozza
Sister Lucia Serafini
Sister Liliana Ugoletti
Sister Mary Boccardo
Father Jean Jacques Luzitu Mukunda

CHRONOLOGY OF KEY EVENTS
IN THE LIFE OF
SAINT JOSEPHINE BAKHITA

1869   Born in Olgossa in Darfur, Sudan.

1874   Bakhita's older sister is kidnapped.

1876   Bakhita is kidnapped.

1876   Sold for the first time to a slave trader. Failed attempt to escape. Sold for the second time to a rich slave trader in El Obeid.

1878   In El Obeid, in the slave trader's house, at the service of his two daughters.

1879   Sold for the third time to a Turkish general in El Obeid.

1882   Journey from El Obeid to Khartoum with the general's entourage and his family.

1882   Sold for the fourth time to the Italian consul Calisto Legnani.

1884   *At the end of the year*: Departure with Legnani (Bakhita is part of his entourage) from Khartoum to Suakin on the Red Sea.

1885   *Mid-March*: departure from Suakin to Genoa, Italy.

1885   *April*: arrival by ship in Genoa; Legnani entrusts Bakhita to the married couple Augusto and Turina Michieli, who live in Zianigo, in the hamlet of Mirano Veneto (outside Venice).

1886   *February 3*: birth of Alice Michieli (Mimmina).

1886   *June*: Augusto Michieli returns to Suakin.

1886 *September:* Turina Michieli goes to Suakin with Mimmina and Bakhita to help her husband who has bought a hotel.

1887 *June:* Turina Michieli returns to Zianigo with Mimmina and Bakhita in order to sell the Michielis' property.

1888 *July 19:* Official sale of the Michielis' real estate, deed no. 2707, registered by Pantoli di Noale.

1888 *November 29:* Bakhita and Mimmina are admitted to the Institute of Catechumens in Venice, run by the Canossian Sisters.

1888 *November/December:* Turina Michieli departs for Suakin.

1889 *November:* Turina returns to Italy with the aim of returning definitively to Suakin with Mimmina and Bakhita.

1889 *November 29:* Bakhita decides to remain in Italy; she is declared legally free by the king's attorney general.

1890 *January 9:* Bakhita receives baptism, confirmation, and first Communion.

1893 *December 7:* Enters the Canossian novitiate at the Institute of Catechumens, under the guidance of Mother Marietta Fabretti.

1895 *June 21:* Friday, feast of the Sacred Heart, Bakhita is clothed in the religious habit.

1896 *December 8:* Sister Bakhita makes her first religious vows at the hands of the superior of the motherhouse in Verona, Mother Anna Previtali.

1902 She is transferred from Venice to the house on Via Fusinato in Schio.

1902 The superior, Mother Margherita Bonotto, assigns Bakhita the task of kitchen helper.

1906 Bakhita's benefactor, Illuminato Checchini, dies in Padua.

1907	Bakhita becomes head cook.
1910	The superior has Mother Teresa Fabris write down the autobiography Bakhita dictates.
1915–1919	The house on Via Fusinato is used as a military hospital. Bakhita serves as cook, sacristan, and nurse's aide.
1922	She overcomes a severe case of bronchial pneumonia that brings her close to death. Experiences some difficulty walking. She is assigned the task of portress.
1927	*August 10*: Makes her perpetual vows in the chapel of the sister house in Mirano Veneto.
1929	*September*: Dictates fragments of her childhood memories to Mother Mariannina Turco intended for the children and grandchildren of her benefactor Illuminato Checchini.
1930	*November 2–4*: Ida Zanolini interviews Bakhita at Sant'Alvise in Venice, at the request of the superior general Maria Cipolla.
1931	*January*: The first installment of *Storia meravigliosa* (*Tale of Wonder*) by Ida Zanolini is published in *Vita Canossiana*, year 5, no. 1.
1931	*December*: The first edition of *Storia meravigliosa* (*Tale of Wonder*) is published.
1933	*May*: Mother Leopolda Benetti, a veteran missionary in China, accompanies Bakhita for three years during numerous trips around Italy on behalf of the missions.
1936	*December 11*: Bakhita, Mother Benetti, and a group of missionaries bound for Addis Ababa are received by Mussolini in the Palazzo Venezia in Rome. During this time Bakhita also meets with Pope Pius XI.

1937–1939	Assigned as portress for the missionary novitiate in Vimercate (Lombardy).
1939	Returns to Schio in poor health. She is not assigned any permanent tasks.
1940–1945	Outbreak of the Second World War. During air raids, the infirm Bakhita does not go to the shelter. All are convinced that with Bakhita in Schio the city will be spared. And so it happens.
1942	After an accidental fall, she can walk only with a cane.
1943	*December 8*: Celebrations for the fiftieth anniversary of religious life.
1943–1944	Walking becomes more difficult; she begins using a wheelchair.
1946	In December she is afflicted with a serious form of bronchial pneumonia and receives extreme unction. Nevertheless, she overcomes the illness.
1947	*February 8*: Dies at 8:10 P.M. Following her death her doctor, Massimino Bertoldi, issues the following diagnosis of her final illness: "Mother Bakhita ultimately suffered from a degenerative myocardial condition leading to a progressive decline in function and low blood pressure. Ultimately, this condition led to acute pulmonary congestion, her immediate cause of death."
1947	*February 11*: Funeral.
1978	*December 1*: Pope John Paul II signs the decree confirming the heroic virtue of Servant of God Josephine Bakhita.
1992	*May 17*: Proclaimed blessed.
2000	*October 1*: Enrolled among the saints.

BIBLIOGRAPHY

Agasso, Domenico. *Un profeta dell'Africa: Daniele Comboni.* Cinisello Balsamo: Edizioni Paoline, 1991.

Albanese, Giulio. "Sudan, il grido dei disperati". *Avvenire,* February 10, 1983.

———. "Sudan, le rotte degli schiavi". *Avvenire,* December 22, 1993.

Arlacchi, Pino. *Schiavi: il nuovo traffico di esseri umani.* Milan: Rizzoli, 1999.

L'attività della Santa Sede 1992–1993. Vatican City: Libreria editrice vaticana.

Bachollet, Raymond, et al. *Négripub.: l'image des Noirs dans la publicité.* Paris: Éditions Somogy, 1992.

Beatificationis et canonizationis Servae Dei Iosephinae Bakhita. Acts of the Ordinary Process in Vicenza (1955–1957) and of the Apostolic Process in Vicenza (1968–1969).

Bhutto, Benazir, and Gro Harlem Brundtland. *Il posto della donna nella società islamica.* International conference on population and development. Cairo, September 5, 1994.

Canossa, Maddalena di. *Memorie: una contemplative nell'azione.* Edited by Elda Pallonara. Milan: Rusconi, 1988. Translated by the Canossian Sisters as *Saint Magdalene of Canossa: Memoirs: A Contemplative in Action.* Rome, Cura Generalizia.

Dagnino, Maria Luisa. *Bakhita racconta la sua storia.* 4th ed. Rome: Figlie della Carità, 1993.

De Laubier, Patrick. *Il pensiero sociale della Chiesa Cattolica.* Milan: Massimo, 1986.

231

Farina, Marcella, and Filomena Rispoli. *Maddalena di Canossa.* Turin: SEI, 1995.

Giacon, Modesto. *Maddalena di Canossa: umiltà nella carità.* Verona: Ordini religiosi canossiani, 1988.

Gibelli, Antonio. *La Grande Guerra degli italiani: 1915–18.* Milan: Sansoni, 1998.

Kurlansky, Mark. *Merluzzo: Storia del pesce che ha cambiato il mondo.* Milan: Oscar saggi Mondadori, 1999.

Mantran, Robert. *Le grandi date dell'Islam.* Cinisello Balsamo: Edizioni Paoline, 1991.

Massarioto, Stefano. *Lunario del Massarioto per il 1993.* Abano Terme: Aldo Francisci, 1992. Reissue of *El Massarioto par el 1891.*

Monici, Claudio. "Loki, capolinea della speranza". *Avvenire.* December 28, 1999.

———. "Niemeri, schiavo senza più Natale". *Avvenire.* December 24, 1999.

———. "Sud Sudan, terra della fede negate". *Avvenire.* January 16, 2000.

Sicari, Antonio Maria. *Ritratti di santi.* Milan: Jaca Book, 1994.

Solari, Patrizia. "Giuseppina Bakhita". In *Santi da scoprire.* 1997.

Sorgi, Claudio. *Il Padre: Josemaría Escrivá de Balaguer.* Casale Monferrato: Piemme, 1992.

Stracca, Silvano. "I cristiani sul calvario in Khartoum". *Avvenire.* February 11, 1993.

La tratta europea degli schiavi d'Africa e il commercio triangolare. Turin: Movimento sviluppo e pace, 1996.

Vantini, Giuseppe. *L'ambiente sociopolitico del Sudan al tempo di Bakhita.* Handout for use by the Canossian Institute.

———. *Bakhita nella sua patria e nei suo tempo.* Handout for use by the Canossian Institute.

Vanzetto, Livio. *Paròn Stefano Massarioto: la crisi della società contadina nel Veneto di fine.* Vicenza: Odeonlibri, 1982.

Villani, Saverio. *L'eccidio di Schio: Una strage inutile.*

Vitapiù. Trimestrale delle Figlie della Carità. Special edition for the beatification of Bakhita. July 1992.

Zanolini, Ida. *Bakhita.* Rome: Figlie della Carità, 1961.

———. *Storia meravigliosa,* 6th ed. Monza: Istituto pavoniano Artigianelli, 1950. Translated by Oliver Todd as *Tale of Wonder: Saint Josephine Bakhita.* 8th ed. Strasbourg: Editions du Signe, 2000.